Panama

Panama

by Byron Augustin

Enchantment of the World
Second Series

Children's Press®

A Division of Scholastic Inc.

New York   Toronto   London   Auckland   Sydney
Mexico City   New Delhi   Hong Kong
Danbury, Connecticut

Frontispiece: Natural beauty of the Panamanian rain forest

Consultant: Kyle Longley, Snell Family Dean's Distinguished Professor, Department of History, Arizona State University, Tempe, AZ

Please note: All statistics are as up-to-date as possible at the time of publication.

Book production by Herman Adler Design

Library of Congress Cataloging-in-Publication Data

Augustin, Byron.
  Panama / by Byron Augustin. — 1st ed.
        p. cm. — (Enchantment of the world. Second series)
  Includes bibliographical references and index.
  ISBN 0-516-23676-8
  1. Panama—Juvenile literature. I. Title. II. Series.
  F1563.2.A842004
  972.87—dc22   2004010165

Acknowledgments

I would like to acknowledge my wife, Rebecca, who supported this project with patience and understanding, and who also edited the text. I am extremely grateful to Skip and Jill Bergen of Gold Coast Travel and Expeditions in Panama. Jill organized a great photo trip, and Skip proved to be a superb professional guide and wonderful travel companion. Skip also provided valuable editing commentary as a forty-eight-year resident of Panama. Jake Kubena, my trusted graduate assistant at Texas State University, completed the tedious task of metric conversions and carefully edited the text. A final note of gratitude is extended to Jesus Prestan, a native Kuna Indian. Working with Panama City Tours, Jesus provided an extraordinary professional tour of Panama City over a three-day period.

This book is dedicated to my parents, Orval and Thelma Augustin; my brothers, Gary and Bruce; my wife, Rebecca; my children, Kelly and Andrew; and my friends, Tim, Gary, Joe, Mike, and Lawrence.

Cover photo:
Kuna mother and
daughter

Contents

CHAPTER

ONE The Link 8

TWO Mountains to Lowlands 14

THREE Nature's Gifts 28

FOUR The Legacy of Time 40

FIVE Building a Nation 62

SIX In Search of Prosperity 72

SEVEN The Melting Pot 84

EIGHT Freedom of Faith 96

NINE A Wealth of Culture 108

TEN Life Is Exciting 118

Coastal town

Timeline **128**

Fast Facts **130**

To Find Out More **134**

Index **136**

Traditional dress

The Link

FOR MILLIONS OF YEARS, THERE WAS NO LAND CONNECTION between South America and Central America. Water flowed freely between the Pacific and the Caribbean Sea, which leads to the Atlantic Ocean. Gradually, nature built the land bridge that connects most nations of the Western Hemisphere. That land bridge would become the Isthmus of Panama, now a major crossroads of physical and cultural diversity.

The land connection provided a pathway for plants and animals from two continents. Birds, mammals, reptiles, insects, trees, flowers, and eventually humans would travel along that fertile trail. Native Americans used Panama as the route to move from North America to South America. Some indigenous people, however, settled permanently in Panama. They took advantage of the rich variety of food provided by the wild plants and animals of the region. They lived in harmony with nature and did little damage to the natural environment for thousands of years.

Spanish explorers arrived at the beginning of the sixteenth century. They did not view Panama as a pathway, but rather as an obstacle. The Spanish sailors were searching for a water route to India. Panama prevented them from reaching the Pacific Ocean

Opposite: **As seen from outer space, Panama links South America to Central America.**

This illustration, entitled *Balboa and the Gold,* **depicts Spanish exploration for gold and silver.**

with their ships. Later, Panama became a valuable possession of Spain after the Spanish discovered large deposits of gold and silver in Peru and Bolivia. Panama provided a route for moving the gold and silver from the Pacific Ocean to the Caribbean Sea and on to the Atlantic and Spain.

After the gold and silver were largely depleted, Spain lost interest in Panama. When the Spanish colonial era ended in 1821, Panama became a part of the independent nation of Colombia. The arrival of the Industrial Revolution and the rapid increase in ocean trade brought a new focus on Panama.

There was increasing interest in many parts of the world for the construction of a canal across Panama. A canal would provide a link rather than a barrier to ocean traffic between the Pacific and the Caribbean Sea and, ultimately, the Atlantic Ocean. The French were the first to attempt to excavate a canal in 1880. Eight years later, after the expenditure of millions of dollars and the loss of thousands of lives, the failed project was abandoned.

The next attempt was made by the United States. In an interference with the sovereign rights of Colombia, in 1903 the United States encouraged Panama to declare its independence from Colombia. The U.S. government,

In the early 1880s France encountered many challenges while excavating the Panama Canal.

led by President Theodore Roosevelt, guaranteed military protection and support for the newly independent Panama. The new nation, in turn, signed a treaty with the United States allowing the United States to build the Panama Canal. The canal was completed in 1914. The completion of the canal introduced an era of U.S. political and economic influence and, at times, interference with Panamanian affairs. On December 31, 1999, the United States returned sovereignty of the Panama Canal to Panama.

The Panama Canal helped make Panama an international crossroads of commercial trade. The country evolved into a market-oriented democracy with a highly developed service sector. Banking, tourism, ship registration, and the world's second largest free trade zone have given Panama a sound financial foundation.

The Panama Canal provides a direct link between the Atlantic and Pacific Oceans for cargo, as well as pleasure ships.

Panamanians are a diverse mix of many peoples.

Ethnic diversity has been guaranteed by the immigration of people from around the globe. These immigrants have helped make Panama a "melting pot" of languages, religions, and cultural traditions. Mosques, cathedrals, synagogues, and temples reflect a variety of religious beliefs and practices. Native American tribes add their unique cultural practices to those of the immigrants.

Culturally, Panama is a society where the family is a great source of security. A good education and literacy for all citizens are prominent goals of the federal government. Panamanians welcome visitors to a nation that has strongly felt passions for music, dance, food, sports, and politics.

Panama is a country with unmatched physical diversity and beauty. Plants and animals that do not exist anywhere else in the world are found in abundance. Tropical rain forests may hold secrets that will unlock cures for devastating diseases.

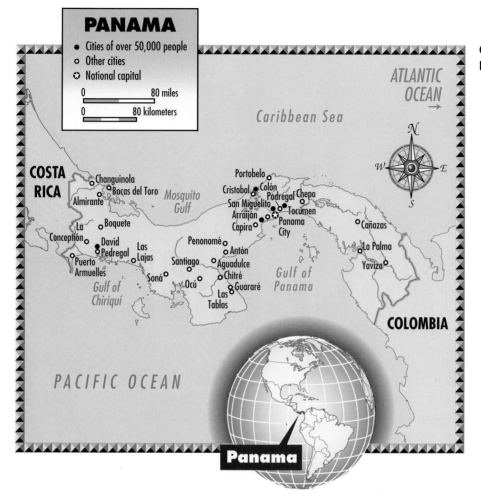

PANAMA

- Cities of over 50,000 people
- Other cities
- National capital

0 — 80 miles
0 — 80 kilometers

ATLANTIC OCEAN →

Caribbean Sea

COSTA RICA

Changuinola
Bocas del Toro
Almirante
Mosquito Gulf

Portobelo
Cristobal · Colón
San Miguelito · Podrégal · Chepo
Arraiján · Tocumen
Capira · Panama City

La Concepción
Boquete
David
Pedregal
Las Lajas
Penonomé
Santiago
Soná
Ocú
Aguadulce
Chitré
Las Tablas
Guararé

Cañazas
La Palma
Yaviza

Gulf of Panama

Puerto Armuelles
Gulf of Chiriquí

PACIFIC OCEAN

COLOMBIA

Panama

High volcanic mountain regions and tropical latitudes provide a climate of eternal spring. White sand beaches, bathed by aqua-blue waters, extend for miles along Panama's coastal regions and offshore islands. Raging white-water rivers plunge from the mountains onto the coastal lowlands. Panama's raw physical beauty has only recently been discovered by tourists. While the new visitors may be surprised, Panamanians have always known that they live in a tropical paradise.

Mountains to Lowlands

14

T HE COUNTRY OF PANAMA IS LOCATED ON ONE OF THE most strategic geographic locations in the world. It serves as the only land connection between Central America and South America. This narrow band of land separates the world's two greatest oceans, the Pacific and the Atlantic, through the Caribbean Sea. The physical landscape in Panama offers visitors a diversity unmatched in most small nations.

Opposite: **Panama's diverse landscape is one of lofty mountains and coastal lowlands.**

The Land Bridge

The narrow strip of land connecting Colombia to Costa Rica is called the Isthmus of Panama. Approximately 190 million years ago, tectonic activity began to push a wedge of rock upward from the ocean floor. Several million years of volcanic action continued to build this potential land link. About 5.7 million years ago, sediment from the volcanic activity filled in the remaining spaces. Finally, a land bridge separated the Pacific Ocean from the Caribbean Sea.

Panama is shaped like an S laying on its side and is slightly smaller than South Carolina. It covers an area of 30,193 square miles (78,200 square kilometers). The country is 480 miles (772 km) in length and ranges from 30 to 75 miles (48 to 120 km) in width. Panama's western border of 205 miles (330 km) is shared with Costa Rica, and its eastern border of 140 miles (225 km) is shared with Colombia. Panama has 1,547 miles (2,490 km) of coastline.

Panama is located in the heart of the tropics. Crossing Panama from the Caribbean Sea to the Gulf of Panama and the Pacific Ocean requires traveling from the northwest to the southeast. This fact created much confusion for European mapmakers in 1513, when Vasco Núñez de Balboa christened the Pacific Ocean, "Mar del Sur," or the South Sea. In Panama City the sun rises in the east over the Pacific Ocean and not the Caribbean Sea.

Panama City at sunrise

Panama's Geographical Features

Area: 30,193 square miles (78,200 sq km)

Highest Elevation: Barú Volcano (Volcán Barú), 11,401 feet (3,475 m)

Lowest Elevation: Sea level along the Caribbean and Pacific coasts

Longest River: Rio Chucunaque, 144 miles (232 km)

Largest Island: Coiba Island (Isla de Coiba), 190 square miles (492 sq km)

Largest Lake: Gatún Lake, 163 square miles (422 sq km)

Coastline: 1,547 miles (2,490 km)

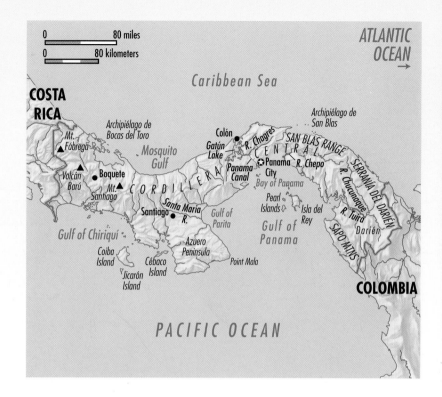

Panama can be divided into three major physical regions. A ridge of mountains and hills serves as a spine passing through the central part of Panama. There are coastal lowlands that vary in width on both the Caribbean and Pacific shorelines. The lowlands make up more than 85 percent of Panama's total land area. The third region is composed of more than 1,500 islands that dot the waters off both coasts.

Mountains

Most of Panama's high, rugged mountains are located west of the Panama Canal. Although the local population has names for small individual ranges, the major complex of mountains is

Volcán Barú is Panama's highest point.

termed the Cordillera Central. The Cordillera Central is volcanic in origin, and its highest elevations are near the border with Costa Rica. Barú Volcano (Volcán Barú), near the city of Boquete, is Panama's highest mountain at 11,401 feet (3,475 meters) above sea level. The rich volcanic soil here has made the region a significant contributor to the agricultural sector of the nation's economy.

The mountains decline in elevation moving eastward toward the middle of Panama. At what was once called the Culebra Cut (now the Gaillard Cut), approximately 12 miles (20 km) northwest of Panama City, is the lowest gap in the mountains. The elevation is only 275 feet (84 m) above sea level. The Culebra Cut provided the best route for both the Panama Canal and the Panama Railroad. East of the Panama Canal most of the mountain spine has been eroded to elevations of less than 3,000 feet (915 m). A small local range of mountains, known as the Serranía del Darién, runs parallel to the border with Colombia.

The Culebra Cut was the most difficult area for canal construction.

Panama's coastal lowlands are most extensively developed along the Pacific coast. Offshore the water is very shallow, seldom reaching depths of more than 300 feet (90 m) in both the Gulf of Panama and the Gulf of Chiriquí. In many areas, mudflats extend more than 43 miles (69 km) off the coast during low tide. This physical condition helps produce extremely high tides of up to 20 feet (6 m). In contrast, the Caribbean coast seldom has tides that measure more than 1 foot (0.3 m) in height. For centuries this tidal difference sustained the belief that the Pacific Ocean was 20 feet (6 m) higher than the Caribbean. Surveyors for the Panama Railroad ended this misconception when they determined that the level of the Caribbean was the same as the Pacific. Cattle grazing, sugarcane cultivation, and rice production are all significant activities on the Pacific coastal lowlands and Azuero Peninsula.

At low tide, Panama's Pacific coast turns to mudflats.

The coastal lowlands on the Caribbean Sea are very narrow, and they contain long stretches of land with sparse populations. Warm, moist air carried by the northeast trade winds produces heavy rainfall along the coast. Bananas and sugarcane are the major crops west of the Panama Canal. East of the canal are some of Panama's most extensive swamps and dense natural rain forests.

The Caribbean coast of Panama is sparsely populated. Pictured here is a small coastal town in the province of Colón.

Islands in the Sun

Few countries have been blessed with the diversity of island geography that Panama possesses. There are more than 1,500 islands in Panama's territorial waters in the Pacific and Caribbean. Some of the islands are volcanic in origin. Others developed from coral. Most visitors to these islands describe them as a tropical paradise.

On the Pacific side, Coiba Island (Isla de Coiba) and the Pearl Islands (Archipiélago de las Perlas) are best known. Coiba Island is Panama's largest island, with an area of 190 square miles (492 sq km). Historically, the island was Panama's most notorious prison camp. In 1991 the island and surrounding waters were declared a national park, Panama's newest.

The Pearl Islands are a group of islands located directly south of Panama City.

The Pearl Islands are comprised of 90 islands and 130 islets (very small islands). During colonial times the Spanish brought black slaves in to dive for pearls in the waters surrounding the islands. The pearls added considerable wealth to Spain. One of the most famous pearls harvested in these waters was the Peregrine Pearl, weighing 31 carats.

On the Caribbean (Atlantic) side of Panama, two groups of islands dominate the landscape: the San Blas Islands (Archipiélago de San Blas) and the Bocas del Toro Islands (Archipiélago de Bocas del Toro). The San Blas Islands are scattered over 100 miles (160 km) to the east of Colón. These 350 islands are home to the Kuna Indians. The Kuna have retained their native language and economic system and are highly independent and politically active.

A canoe off the shore of Acuatupo Island, home to the Kuna Indians in the San Blas Islands.

The Bocas del Toro Islands are situated off the northwest coast of Panama near the Costa Rican border. Christopher Columbus anchored in these waters in 1502 while he repaired his boats. Later, British pirates hid out among the islands while raiding Spanish galleons laden with silver and gold. At the beginning of the twentieth century, the town of Bocas del Toro was selected as the headquarters of the U.S.-owned United Fruit Company and grew to 25,000 residents. The United Fruit Company exported bananas and at one time was the largest agricultural company in the world. Today, the islands have become a prime real estate market for retiring Americans as well as a tourist hot spot for diving and snorkeling.

Climate

Panama has a tropical maritime climate that is hot and humid most of the year. The country's location near the equator means that the four seasons of spring, summer, fall, and winter simply merge into a yearlong summer. The average temperature difference between the warmest and coldest months is less than 15 degrees Fahrenheit (9 degrees Celsius) across most of the country. In the lowlands, daytime temperatures usually are in the high 80s and low 90s in degrees Fahrenheit (30°C) and rarely cooler than 70°F (21°C) at night. The only break from the consistently high temperatures is found in the mountains of the west, where elevations between 5,000 to 10,000 feet (1,500 to 3,050 m) produce a pleasant climate. The city of Boquete, near Barú Volcano, has been nicknamed "The City of Eternal Spring." Here, the temperatures range between 50°F and 64°F (10°C to 18°C) throughout the year.

Seasons in Panama are not determined by temperature, but rather by precipitation. There are just two seasons—a wet season and a dry season. The long wet season begins in May and continues to mid-December. During the wet season it rains almost every day. There is a short dry season from mid-December to May.

The thunderstorms that impact Panama reflect the raw power of nature. The day usually begins with scattered clouds. In the early afternoon the clouds begin to form into towering, massive thunderheads. The sky darkens and it becomes very quiet. The birds stop chirping, and it seems as if all noise has been snuffed out. Suddenly there is an unspeakably blinding flash of lightning; then the stillness is broken immediately by an ear-shattering clap of thunder. The storm has begun.

For the next hour or two, it appears as if the sky has opened and is dumping buckets of water on the landscape. Streets fill with water and rivers become raging torrents, overflowing their banks. Then, just as quickly as the storm began, it is over. The sun breaks through the clouds, framing golden droplets of water on the luxurious rain forest vegetation.

Downpours are common during the wet season.

The Chagres River is part of the Panama Canal system. On its northwest journey it is dammed to form Gatún Lake.

Rainfall patterns in Panama are consistent neither from location to location nor from year to year. The total amount of precipitation decreases from north to south across Panama. Colón on the northern coast averages 126 inches (320 centimeters) a year. Barro Colorado Island, located in Gatún Lake, receives an average of 106 inches (269 cm) each year. Panama City on the south coast has an average annual precipitation of 75 inches (190 cm). Barro Colorado Island is an example of how the amount of rainfall can change from year to year in the same location. In 1981 the official weather station recorded 176 inches (447 cm) of rainfall. In 1997 only 67 inches (170 cm) of precipitation fell at the same weather station. That is a difference of more than 250 percent between the wettest and driest years!

The large amounts of precipitation that fall across Panama have helped create nearly 500 rivers. More than 150 rivers flow into the Caribbean, and between 300 and 350 empty into the Pacific. The Río Tuira, Río Chucunaque, and Río Chepo are among the major Pacific-flowing rivers. The Río Chepo is an important source of hydroelectric power. The Río Chagres is the longest and most dominant river flowing toward the Caribbean. Taming the Chagres to provide freshwater for the Panama Canal's Lake Gatún was a difficult engineering task. After completion of the canal, the Río Chagres became the only river in the world whose water flows into two oceans.

A Look at Panama's Cities

The city of Colón (above) was founded in 1850 by the builders of the Panama Railroad. The original name of the city was Aspinwall. In 1890 the city was renamed Colón to honor Christopher Columbus. (Colón is Spanish for the word *Columbus*.) The city is located on Manzanillo Island, just 13 feet (4 m) above sea level. The average temperature in both January and July is 80°F (26.7°C). Colón has the largest black population of any community in Panama. The blacks are descendents of the workers who helped dig the Panama Canal. The second largest free trade zone in the world is located in Colón. Recently, Colón has become an important stop for cruise ships.

The city of Boquete was founded in 1911 and settled by Panamanians, Swiss, Yugoslavs, Swedes, and Germans. The city's elevation is 4,000 feet (1,220 m) above sea level. It has an average January temperature of 66°F (18.8°C) and an average July temperature of 68°F (20°C). Residents refer to Boquete as a place of "eternal spring" because of its climatic conditions. The city is known for its abundance of flowers (below) and prosperous coffee plantations. Each January thousands of tourists descend upon the city to participate in the annual Flower and Coffee Festival.

Santiago is Panama's fourth largest city. It is located in central Panama on the Pacific lowlands at an elevation of 288 feet (88 m) above sea level. The average January temperature is 82°F (27.8°C), while the average July temperature is 81°F (27.2°C). Santiago is an important stop on the Pan American Highway and is the capital of Veraguas Province. The city is a significant communications and commercial center.

Nature's Gifts

PANAMA POSSESSES SOME OF THE MOST PRECIOUS GIFTS OF our natural world. The diversity of plant and animal life is almost beyond belief. The country's location between the ecosystems of North America and South America has brought about a mixing of species that is truly unique. Scientists from across the globe have been visiting Panama for decades to study its rich natural environment. They have discovered many species of plants and animals not found at any other location on the globe.

Before the Spanish arrived in Panama in 1501, much of the country was covered with dense tropical rain forests. Under Spanish colonial rule, the forests were greatly reduced, the result of clearing for farmland and lumber. At the beginning of the twentieth century, deforestation began to accelerate. By 1970, less than half of Panama was covered by forests. Today a mere 32 percent of the magnificent original forests remain, mainly located in the eastern half of Panama.

Shades of Green

Panama has more than 10,000 different species of plants, most of which can be found in the remaining rain forests. Trees dominate the landscape, soaring to

Opposite: **Panama's wildlife is one of diversity and beauty. Here, two parrots perch among the trees.**

Sunlight searches for an opening in the dense growth of the rain forest.

heights of 120 to 130 feet (37 to 40 m). More than 1,500 species of trees have been identified. The trees produce a canopy over the forest floor that shuts out sunlight and restricts other plant growth. Still, more than 678 species of ferns survive in the limited light available. Scores of vines snake up the trunks of the trees to reach sunlight near the top of the canopy. Epiphytes, such as orchids, attach themselves to the trees and draw their food and water supply from the host trees. Panama has more than 1,200 varieties of orchids. It is not unusual to find twenty different species of orchids growing on a single tree.

The trees in the forests have local names such as Barrigon, Jobo, Guayacan, Cabresto, and Negrito. Rain forest trees provide fruit for humans and animals. Their bark is used for medicines, their leaves are woven into hats and baskets, and the trees are harvested for lumber. They also provide an important habitat for birds, mammals, reptiles, and insects.

The plants and trees of the rain forests are treasures that need to be preserved for all mankind. Almost 40 percent of all prescription medicines in the United States have active ingredients taken from rain forest plants. The United States National Cancer Institute believes that rain forest plants hold the greatest potential for providing cures for various cancers.

Nature's Zoo

Panama is blessed with a diversity of animal life seldom found in a country its size. Representatives of the animal kingdom range from tiny insects to the largest land mammal found between Mexico and South America. There are 225 species of mammals, 143 species of amphibians, and 214 species of reptiles, including some of the most poisonous snakes in the world. The openly aggressive bushmaster can reach lengths of more than 13 feet (4 m). It is the largest poisonous snake in the Americas. More than 80 percent of its victims do not survive its bite. Panama is a bird watcher's paradise, with more

The bushmaster is one of the largest venomous snakes living in the rain forest.

than 950 documented species of birds. Like other areas of the world, however, insects dominate the environment with more than 160,000 different species.

The roar of the jaguar or the sudden sight of the deadly bushmaster can strike fear in the hearts of most people. However, it was the tiny insects of Panama that posed the greatest threat to the early visitors. The Spaniards called them *bichos*, a term that included ticks, chiggers, spiders, ants, flies, scorpions, and mosquitoes.

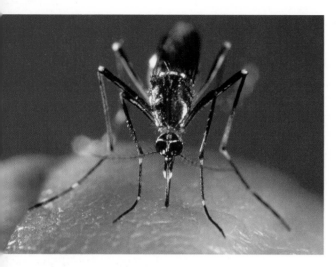

This mosquito, the *Aedes aegypti*, carries yellow fever, a disease deadly to humans.

There are more than 2,500 species of mosquitoes worldwide. In Panama, two species have been a continuous health threat to humans. The *Stegomyia fasiata* (sometimes called *Aedes aegypti*) carries yellow fever. The Anopheles mosquito is the carrier of deadly malaria. During the French and American construction of the Panama Canal an estimated total of 20,000 to 25,000 workers died from malaria and yellow fever. While most areas of the country are safe today, some remote areas still have mosquitoes that carry the diseases.

Feathered Friends

The lofty canopies of Panama's rain forests are filled with the shrill cries, chirping, and hypnotizing harmonies of a multitude of birds. There are more species of birds in Panama than there are in the United States and Canada combined. Scarlet macaws breed on Coiba Island. Parrots, toucans, crested eagles, and other magnificent species are widely distributed across the country.

Bird life abounds in Panama. This is a keel-billed toucan.

The National Bird

The harpy eagle (above) is the national bird of Panama. It is the world's largest and most powerful eagle. The female is larger than the male. It stands nearly 3 feet (1 m) in height and may have a wingspan of up to 7 feet (2.2 m). It has powerful talons up to 5 inches (13 cm) in length, as long as the claws of a grizzly bear. It is a meat eater and feeds on monkeys, sloths, iguanas, opossums, and large rodents.

A male quetzal adds color to the cloud forests in Panama.

The strikingly beautiful quetzal inhabits the cloud forests of northwestern Panama. Cloud forests develop in mountains where the higher elevations result in cooling, and condensation forms moisture-rich clouds. The male quetzal has brilliant red breast feathers and emerald green back feathers. Its tail feathers may reach 3 feet (1 m) in length and are iridescent blue and green in color. Tail feathers from the quetzal were used to make the headdress for Montezuma, the famous Aztec king.

A three-toed sloth hangs from a cecropia tree in Panama's rain forest.

The mammals of Panama include the slow-moving sloths, tiny marmosets, and monkeys that live in the canopies of the rain forest. Giant anteaters and tapirs search for fruit and leaves on the forest floor. The tapir, which is the largest mammal in Panama, can weigh up to 700 pounds (318 kilograms). Capybara, the world's largest rodents, move in groups along the banks of rain forest rivers.

The most majestic of the rain forest mammals are the cats, including jaguars, pumas, ocelots, margay cats, and jaguarundi. Environmentalists judge the health of the rain forest wildlife by the presence of big cats. In Panama there is major concern for the jaguars as their habitat grows smaller each year and poachers shoot them for their beautiful hides.

Jaguarundi are found in dense forest areas, often near rivers. They are very good climbers and swimmers.

A Kuna Indian paddles his canoe through a mangrove forest.

Land Meets Water

Panama's shoreline, offshore islands, and coastal waters are teeming with life. Mangrove forests are abundant on both the Pacific and Caribbean coasts. Almost half of the mangrove forests are concentrated along the Gulf of San Miguel in southeastern Panama. These mangroves serve as important nurseries for saltwater shrimp, which are one of Panama's significant exports. In 1999 Panama was the world's third largest exporter of shrimp.

Some of the best coral reefs in Central America are found in Panamanian waters. The largest is located near Coiba Island in the Pacific Ocean. There are also well-developed coral reefs near the islands of Bocas del Toro and the San Blas Islands in the Caribbean Sea. Coral reefs have been described as the "rain forests of the oceans" because of the rich and abundant life they harbor. More than two hundred species of marine fish are found among the coral reefs.

This photo shows the effects of deforestation in the Panama rain forest.

A Threatened Environment

Panama is a small country, and many of its citizens are poor. There are demands on the government of Panama to harvest its natural resources. There is pressure to open the land to large international companies for development. It is difficult for the country to balance its economic interests with its environmental responsibilities.

The greatest environmental threat in Panama is deforestation. Panama's tropical rain forests are the nation's crown jewels. The rain forests are under attack. Subsistence farmers are cutting down the trees so that they can grow enough crops or raise enough livestock to try to feed their families. Lumber companies are cutting the best and biggest trees to sell the rare woods as exports. Mining companies are stripping the land of the trees to dig for copper and gold. Roads are being built to provide access to the forests. All of these activities destroy habitat that is critical for the existence of wildlife.

Some environmentalists predict that the destruction of the rain forests could lead to a climatic change in Panama. They believe that if the forests are removed, less rain will fall. If this occurs, there might not be enough freshwater to operate the Panama Canal. It requires at least 52,000,000 gallons (197,000,000 liters) of freshwater for just one ship to pass through the canal.

Protecting the Innocent

Many people in Panama are working hard to try to protect their natural treasures. The country has established fourteen national parks, a dozen forest reserves, and ten wildlife sanctuaries. Darién National Park is one of the greatest wilderness

Darién National Park is one of the largest reserves in the world.

areas in the world. The park covers 1,430,740 acres (579,000 hectares). Some areas of the park have never been explored by humans. The United Nations Educational, Scientific and Cultural Organization (UNESCO) listed the park as a World Heritage Site in 1981. In 1983, the United Nations listed the park as a United Nations Biosphere Reserve.

The Chagres National Park covers 318,766 acres (129,000 ha) in the drainage basin of the Chagres River. The river, by way of Gatún Lake, provides 80 percent of the freshwater for the Panama Canal and all of the drinking water for Panama City. Amistad National Park and Portobelo National Park are also listed as UNESCO World Heritage Sites. Coiba Island National Park is one of the largest marine parks in the world.

One of the most interesting scientific research sites in the world is the Barro Colorado Nature Monument. The biological reserve is a 4,000-acre (1,620-ha) island in the middle of Gatún Lake. The lake was formed in 1913 when the Chagres River was dammed to provide freshwater to the Panama Canal. At that time, the island was part of the Canal Zone administered by the United States.

In 1923 a group of scientists petitioned the governor of the Canal Zone to set the island aside for research. In 1946 the island was turned over to the Smithsonian Institute to manage. The project became one of the first protected tropical rain forests in the Western Hemisphere.

Barro Colorado Island is one of Earth's most exciting natural research laboratories. Scientists arrive from everywhere to study the undisturbed rain forest. Their research has proved

that there are more species of plants on this 6 square mile (15.5 sq km) island than there are on the entire European continent. In 1981 a tree that reached more than 100 feet (30.5 m) in height was discovered. The tree's species was previously unknown to science.

The rain forest of Gatún Lake was the first protected in the Western Hemisphere.

The Legacy
of Time

H ISTORY BOOKS OFTEN GIVE credit to Europeans for "discovering" the New World. In reality, Native Americans had been living in the Americas for thousands of years before the arrival of Columbus. Most archaeologists believe that the earliest human occupation of Panama occurred between 10,000 and 12,000 years ago. Scientists speculate that the first migrants crossed the Bering land bridge from Asia. They traveled slowly southward through North America and into Central America.

When the Spanish arrived on that tropical shore at the beginning of the sixteenth century, there may have been as many as sixty different native tribes in Panama. Their population at that time was estimated to be 500,000. The Native Americans were found dwelling on the coastal lowlands, offshore islands, and along the riverbanks of the rain forests.

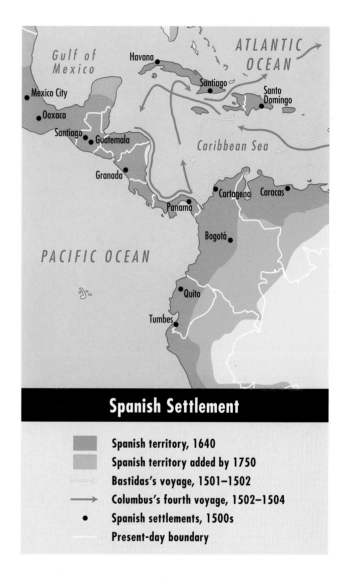

Spanish Settlement

	Spanish territory, 1640
	Spanish territory added by 1750
	Bastidas's voyage, 1501–1502
	Columbus's fourth voyage, 1502–1504
•	Spanish settlements, 1500s
	Present-day boundary

Opposite: **English navigator Sir Francis Drake sailed the waters off Panama in 1573. This illustration shows Drake with a Native Indian from Panama.**

In 1501 Rodrigo de Bastidas arrived off the eastern coast of Panama. He is credited with the "discovery" of Panama. The following year, on October 5, 1502, Christopher Columbus arrived in the Bocas del Toro Islands along the northwest coast of Panama. It was Columbus's fourth trip to the New World. He spent a little more than six months exploring Panama's northern coast. On April 16, 1503, he returned to Hispaniola (the island with Haiti and the Dominican Republic), then back to Spain. This was his final trip to the New World.

In 1508 the king of Spain named the Panama region Castilla del Oro, or Castle of Gold. He appointed Diego de Nicuesa as its first governor. Two years later, in 1510, Martín Fernández de

Christopher Columbus sailed to Panama and spent several months exploring its northern coast.

Enciso, a wealthy lawyer, would found the village of Antigua (Santa María de la Antigua del Darién). Antigua became the first permanent European settlement in Central America.

Antigua flourished and became a successful colony. The colonists rejected the leaders sent from Spain and elected Vasco Núñez de Balboa as the *alcalde* (mayor) of Antigua. The popular mayor was a bit of a scoundrel, having fled Hispaniola to avoid paying large debts. With this unpleasantness behind him, however, he proved to be a very able administrator.

Balboa was a true explorer at heart. He had heard rumors of a great sea across the mountains from Antigua. On September 1, 1513, Balboa left Antigua and proceeded in a southerly direction. His group consisted of 190 Spaniards and 1,000 local natives. They hacked their way through the jungle, enduring incredible hardship on their trek to the sea. Four weeks later, on September 29, 1513, the tired explorers walked into the Pacific Ocean. Balboa raised his sword above his head and claimed the ocean and all its surrounding land in the name of Spain. He was the first European to view the Pacific Ocean. Accompanying Balboa on the difficult trip was an obscure *conquistador*, or leader, by the name of Francisco Pizarro, who later would conquer the Inca Empire.

This painting by Clyde O. De Land depicts Spanish explorer Balboa seeing the Pacific Ocean for the first time.

Conqueror of the Incas

Francisco Pizarro remembered his first sighting of the Pacific Ocean with Balboa. In 1532 he led an expedition to Peru and captured the powerful Inca chief Atahualpa (left). Over the next three hundred years, the Spanish would ravage the gold and silver deposits of the Inca Empire. Almost all of these treasures would pass through Panama on their way to Spain. Panama would become one of the most important crossroads in the world.

Pedro Arias Dávila founded Panama City in 1519.

Six months after Balboa's return, a new Spanish governor arrived in Antigua. His name was Pedro Arias Dávila (Pedrarias). He was best known by his nickname, Pedro the Cruel. He had an unpleasant personality and was a liar who vowed revenge against any person who dared to oppose him. Pedrarias immediately viewed Balboa as a threat to his governorship. He hatched a plot to remove the popular mayor of Antigua. In 1517 he had Balboa arrested on false charges. Before the trial even started, Pedrarias arranged the verdict with the judge, the prosecutor, and several false witnesses. Balboa was found guilty of treason and was quickly beheaded.

Pedrarias governed Panama from 1514 until 1526. His most significant political decision

Portobelo

Portobelo became the major Atlantic port for gold and silver. In 1597 the Spanish began constructing four strong fortresses overlooking the harbor. In 1630, they built a stone customs house to hold the gold and silver treasure for shipment to Spain. Portobelo became a favorite target of pirates and of the British navy. In 1739 British admiral Edward Vernon destroyed the fortifications at Portobelo.

The city hosted at least one major trade fair each year. The fairs would begin when a fleet of merchant ships arrived loaded with goods from Spain. The goods were traded for gold and silver. Individual fairs lasted forty to sixty days and were times of great festivity.

was to move the capital from Antigua to Panama, later named Panama City. Panama City was founded as Nuestra Señora de la Asunción de Panama on August 15, 1519. Earlier, it had been the site of an Indian fishing village that the natives called *Panama*. In the Indian language, Panama meant "abundance of fish." Pedrarias's time as governor is one of the darkest periods in Panama's history. His greed led him on a ruthless search for gold. He was cruel and brutal in his treatment of the Native Americans. His legacy was his responsibility for the extermination of a large percentage of the indigenous population.

A River of Silver and Gold

The search for riches extended for long distances southward. The gold of the Inca Empire and the silver of Bolivia's incredibly rich Cerro Rico Mountain moved by ship from Lima, Peru, to Panama City. The precious metals were then moved overland to Nombre de Dios and Portobelo. They were stored at these sites until they could be shipped to Spain on Spanish galleons.

On the Pacific coast, Panama City prospered. Wealthy merchants built fine stone houses and contributed generously for the construction of religious buildings. Panama's fine cathedral was one of the most imposing religious structures in the New World. The city provided an elegant setting for a wealthy Spanish aristocracy.

On January 18, 1671, the British buccaneer Sir Henry Morgan brought an end to the tranquil lives of Panama City's residents. Morgan and his ill-mannered and violent gang of thugs laid siege to the city. They harassed, tortured, and killed many of the city's citizens for more than a month before leaving. Fire destroyed most of the elegant buildings, including the magnificent cathedral. The destruction was so

Sir Henry Morgan and his men capture Panama City.

complete that the capital city was abandoned and moved to a more defendable site 5 miles (8 km) from the original location.

Beginning in 1567 Spain decreed the Viceroyalty of Peru to be responsible for governing Panama. In 1739 those political responsibilities shifted to the Viceroyalty of New Granada (in present-day Colombia). By this date, the gold and silver trade was a trickle compared with the flooded past, and Panama became a backwater of Spanish interests.

The Liberator

By the start of the nineteenth century, inhabitants of New Granada had tired of the bureaucracy and inconsistencies of Spanish rule. They dreamed of independence. Simón Bolívar, a member of an aristocratic family from Venezuela, led the independence movement. In August 1819

AUDIENCIA OF CUBA
BRITISH TERRITORY
VICEROYALTY OF NEW SPAIN
Gulf of Mexico
AUDENCIA OF CUBA
ATLANTIC OCEAN
Caribbean Sea
VICEROYALTY OF NEW GRANADA
GUIANA
PACIFIC OCEAN
VICEROYALTY OF BRAZIL
VICEROYALTY OF PERU
VICEROYALTY OF LA PLATA
ATLANTIC OCEAN
PATAGONIA

Colonial Latin America, 1780

British colonies
Portuguese colonies
Spanish colonies
Uncolonized territory
Administrative boundaries, 1780

General Simón Bolívar led his troops in a fight for Colombian independence.

the Spanish were defeated at Boyacá by revolutionary troops led by Bolívar and General Francisco de Paula Santander. In 1821 Panama became a part of the newly independent Republic of Gran Colombia. The new nation included Venezuela, Colombia, and Panama. Ecuador joined in 1822. Friction between the countries, however, led Venezuela and Ecuador to withdraw from the union in 1830.

In 1831 the Republic of New Granada was formed. It included only Colombia and Panama. In 1886 the nation changed its name to the Republic of Colombia. Panama was isolated from the capital city of Bogotá by distance and poor travel connections. The Colombians paid little attention to the remote political department of Panama.

The Iron Horse

During the early to mid-1800s the United States acquired vast areas of western territory through aggressive military action and land purchases, but it was difficult for most Americans to get there. The country was looking for a way to reach California from the eastern seaboard without crossing the immense continent. In 1846 Benjamin Bidlack, a U.S. diplomat, signed a treaty with President Tomás Cipriano de Mosquera of New Granada. The treaty guaranteed the United

States the exclusive right of transit across the Isthmus of Panama. The Panama Railroad Company was formed in New York City and secured financing to build a railroad.

Construction began in May 1850 on Manzanillo Island, the site of the present-day city of Colón. It was one of the most difficult engineering tasks ever undertaken. Workers had to conquer swamps, raging rivers, sticky mud, and steep canyons. The railroad was only 47.5 miles (76.4 km) long, but more than 300 bridges and culverts were necessary for completion. Poisonous snakes, cholera, dysentery, yellow fever, and malaria took a high toll on the workers. Although no records were kept, reliable estimates suggest that more than 6,000 workers died during construction.

The last rail was laid on January 27, 1855. The following day a smoke-puffing engine left Aspinwall (Colón) for Panama City. It was the world's first transcontinental railroad journey. The Panama Railroad became one of the most profitable railroads ever built. It also played a critical role in the construction of the Panama Canal.

The Panama Railroad was a vital element in the construction of the Panama Canal. It transported men, food, and supplies to worksites.

Interest in a navigable canal across the Isthmus of Panama was first expressed in 1534. Emperor Charles V ordered surveys to determine if a canal was feasible. His chief surveyor reported that "no prince in the world had enough money and power to unite the world's two greatest oceans." Later there would be other vocal supporters for a canal, including Benjamin Franklin. Simón Bolívar hired engineers to survey for a potential canal route. It was the French, however, who would make the first attempt to actually dig a canal.

In 1878 Lieutenant Lucien Napoleon Bonaparte Wyse secured an exclusive agreement with the government of the Republic of Colombia to build a canal. A French company headed by Ferdinand-Marie de Lesseps was established to carry out the task. De Lesseps was one of the most popular men in France because he had successfully completed construction of the Suez Canal in Egypt. He was energetic, handsome, charismatic, and a spectacular promoter. He quickly raised millions of dollars for the project, mostly from small French investors.

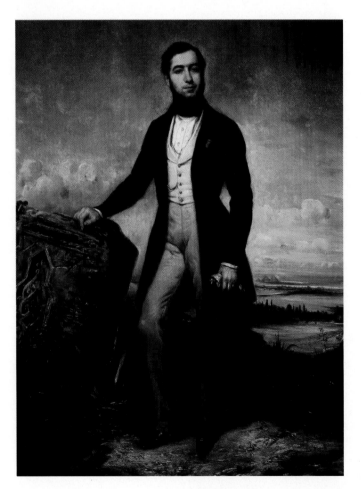

Though Ferdinand de Lesseps gained great fame after completing the Suez Canal in Egypt, his attempt at the Panama Canal ended in failure.

De Lesseps was insistent that the canal should be a sea-level canal. That concept was opposed by many engineers. Nonetheless, construction began formally on January 1, 1880. It ended in December 1888 when the company declared itself bankrupt. Thousands of small French investors lost their life's savings.

Laborers at the Culebra Cut take a break from construction.

De Lesseps had underestimated the overwhelming challenges of Panama's physical environment. More than 20,000 workers died, primarily of malaria and yellow fever. Also, heavy rainfall caused flooding and landslides. It was difficult to transport supplies to such a remote region. Finally, De Lesseps had badly misjudged the costs of the project. His insistence on a sea-level canal had been a fatal technical error from the beginning. Convicted of embezzlement, de Lesseps died in disgrace at his French country home.

In 1894 the French reorganized the remains of the project and formed the Compagnie Nouvelle du Canal de Panama. The new company recognized that the canal would require a series of locks instead of a sea-level passage. This second effort also proved futile, however, and in 1904 the French sold their rights to the United States for $40,000,000.

A Time of Trouble

The second half of the nineteenth century was characterized by political turmoil in Panama and Colombia. There were frequent hostile changes in the administration of the government, which led to civil instability. There were five unsuccessful attempts by Panama to secede from the Republic of Colombia. The United States routinely intervened in Panama's political affairs by sending troops to protect U.S. interests. Political strife in Colombia spread to Panama and caused great unrest.

In 1899 violent conflict between the Liberal and the Conservative Parties in Colombia broke out in an open civil war. The conflict was fought almost entirely in Panama and lasted until 1902. It is known historically as "The Thousand Day War." Approximately 100,000 citizens died in the conflict. A movement for independence was rising in Panama.

Stars and Stripes

Meanwhile, in the United States there was a strong interest in the construction of a canal to connect the Atlantic Ocean to the Pacific Ocean. This movement was led by President Theodore Roosevelt, who thought a canal would favor U.S. sea power and make the nation a world leader. In January 1903, diplomats from the United States and Colombia signed the Hay-Herran Treaty. In the treaty, Colombia granted consent for the United States to have a 100-year lease on a 6-mile- (10-km-) wide strip of land through central Panama for canal construction. The Colombian Senate refused to ratify the treaty, however. The United States did not give up and encouraged the Panamanians to declare their independence. Behind the scenes, U.S. government officials promised quick recognition of the new Republic of Panama and immediate military support.

On November 3, 1903, Panama declared its independence from Colombia. U.S. navy gunboats and troops effectively prevented Colombian troops from moving to Panama City to put down the insurrection. The next day the United States formally recognized the new Republic of Panama. Dr. Manuel Amador Guerrero was selected as the first president. The citizens of Colombia were furious. There were riots in the streets of Bogotá. Political relations with Colombia, as well as most of Latin America, had been seriously damaged.

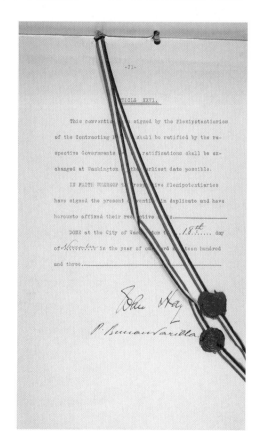

The Hay–Bunau-Varilla Treaty granted the United States use and control of a zone for the Panama Canal.

A New Treaty

The United States immediately opened discussions for a different canal treaty with the new government of Panama. The Panamanians appointed a French citizen, Philippe Bunau-Varilla, to represent them in the negotiations. Bunau-Varilla was a poor choice. He was more interested in protecting previous French investments than in securing a fair treaty for Panama. The United States was not about to give up. The result of negotiations was the Hay–Bunau-Varilla Treaty of November 18, 1903, which

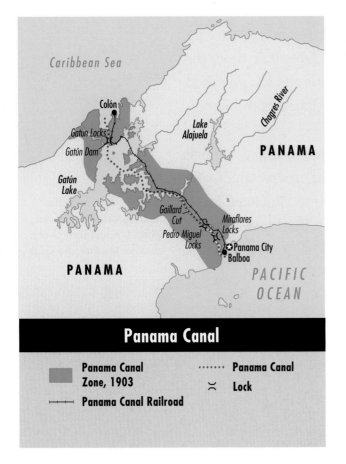

Panama Canal

- Panama Canal Zone, 1903
- Panama Canal Railroad
- ······ Panama Canal
- ⋈ Lock

greatly favored the United States. The treaty gave the United States exclusive rights to a 50-mile (80-km) strip of land, 10 miles (16 km) in width, through the heart of Panama. It created a Canal Zone that was the sovereign property of the United States in perpetuity (forever). In return, Panama received a paltry $10,000,000 and an annual payment of $250,000.

Let the Dirt Fly

U.S. construction of the Panama Canal began in 1904. The canal was completed in 1914 at a cost of $387,000,000. Workers came from almost every country in the world. The greatest numbers were black laborers from Barbados and other West Indies islands. The workers were faced with the same dangers that had devastated the French workers. Malaria and yellow fever still posed the greatest threat to life. Colonel William Crawford Gorgas is given credit for resolving this crisis by ridding the Canal Zone of most of the mosquitoes that carried the diseases. The army doctor organized patrols to empty any containers holding stagnant water where mosquitoes could breed. In addition, chemicals were sprayed on ditches and trenches with standing water to kill the mosquitoes. His pioneering work contributed to saving thousands of lives in the Canal Zone.

Brilliant engineering helped conquer the physical challenges that Panama presented. In order to tame the unruly Chagres River, the Gatún Dam was constructed to form Gatún Lake. When the dam was completed, Gatún Lake became the largest man-made lake in the world, providing water needed to operate the canal locks. Ships now travel 23.5 miles (37.8 km) through the lake. Giant steam shovels gouged a channel through the Gaillard (Culebra) Cut. This was the most difficult and frustrating task in the canal construction because of continual landslides.

Engineers had abandoned the idea of a sea-level canal and instead built a series of locks at Gatún, Pedro Miguel, and Miraflores. The locks fill with water, lift the ships from sea level to Lake Gatún, and lower them back to sea level by releasing water. John Stevens and Lieutenant Colonel George

Workers dig by hand during construction of the Culebra Cut.

An oil tanker enters the Miraflores lock. Notice the lower water level in the right-hand side.

The Legacy of Time **55**

Washington Goethals were the two most prominent engineers to manage the project. When the canal was completed, many professionals declared that it was the greatest engineering accomplishment of all time.

Troubled Waters

The Hay–Bunau-Varilla Treaty made the nation of Panama a virtual protectorate of the United States. Many Panamanians, however, resented the presence of U.S. troops on Panama's soil. They felt that Canal Zone officials and employees were arrogant and acted superior in their relations with them. While grim poverty was a fact of life for many Panamanians, U.S. citizens appeared to live the "good life" in the Canal Zone. Over the years, this growing resentment of the Americans' lifestyle contributed to a surge of Panamanian nationalism.

By the middle of the twentieth century, political instability in the Panamanian government had created social and economic problems. There were four different presidents in 1949 alone. In 1955 President José Antonio Remón was assassinated. On January 9, 1964, years of humiliation and growing Panamanian nationalism led to major riots in the Canal Zone. A long-standing disagreement regarding the flying of the American and Panamanian flags in the zone triggered demonstrations that turned violent. In the end, more than twenty Panamanian citizens died in the riots and millions of dollars of damage was inflicted on U.S. property. In Panama, January 9 has been declared Martyr's Day, a national holiday.

Democracy to Dictatorship

In 1968 President Arnulfo Arias Madrid was removed from office by the Panamanian military. He was replaced by Brigadier General Omar Torrijos Herrera, the commander of the National Guard, in a military coup d'état. Torrijos was a corrupt, iron-fisted dictator who treated opponents harshly. Nevertheless, he promoted health care, housing, and education programs that benefited the poor. For many Panamanians, living conditions were better under the dictator. Torrijos also gained considerable public support for his nationalistic foreign policy and relentless criticism of the U.S. presence in Panama.

Brigadier General Omar Torrijos Herrera

The most powerful leader during the past century of Panamanian politics was the military dictator General Omar Torrijos Herrera. Torrijos was one of twelve children from a lower middle-class mestizo (mixed Native American and white ancestry) family. At eighteen years of age he enrolled in a military academy in El Salvador. Later he joined the Panama National Police Force. He was appointed Executive Secretary of the Panama National Guard in 1966.

Torrijos rapidly gained a strong following among the members of the National Guard, who were mostly black and mestizo. In 1968 he became the military dictator of Panama. He appointed friends to high-level government positions, where they stole freely from the national treasury. Torrijos also overlooked the fact that members of the National Guard engaged in illegal drug trafficking and weapons sales. While he was dictator, he changed the name of the National Guard to the Panamanian Defense Forces (PDF). He skillfully built the PDF into the most powerful political organization in Panama.

In 1977 Torrijos successfully negotiated new treaties with the United States regarding the Canal Zone. The treaties called for the gradual takeover of the Canal Zone by Panama over a twenty-year period beginning in 1979. They guaranteed that the canal would remain neutral. In addition, the United States could intervene militarily if the security of the canal were threatened.

Drugs and Money

In 1981 General Torrijos was killed in an airplane crash. After his death, an elected civilian government emerged. Behind the scenes, however, it was apparent that the military still dominated Panamanian political life. General Manuel Noriega controlled both the Panama Defense Forces and the civilian government. He surrounded himself with thugs and evolved into a political strongman.

Initially Noriega faked a willingness to cooperate with U.S. efforts to halt the drug traffic in Panama. He was actually paid by the Central Intelligence Agency (CIA) to inform on Colombian

Manuel Noriega's activities were unacceptable to U.S. law enforcement, which ultimately led to his capture and imprisonment.

drug dealers. His short-lived cooperation with the United States was replaced with open criticism of the American government. In 1987 Noriega cronies attacked the U.S. embassy. In retaliation, the United States froze all economic and military assistance to Panama. In February 1988, General Noriega was indicted by U.S. courts on drug-trafficking charges. In May 1989, when national elections were held, Panamanians voted 3 to 1 against Noriega's hand-picked candidates. Noriega stepped in and nullified the election. Massive citizen unrest and the death of a U.S. soldier in Panama led to a strong reaction from the United States.

On December 20, 1989, President George H.W. Bush ordered the U.S. military to invade Panama to restore order and protect U.S. lives and property. The action was termed "Operation Just Cause." There were 27,000 U.S. troops

In 1989, President George H.W. Bush deployed U.S. troops to capture Noriega and bring order and peace to Panama.

involved in the invasion. The official death toll was 23 Americans and 254 Panamanians. Many observers, however, believe that the Panamanian death toll was actually between 1,000 and 2,000, most of whom were civilians. Noriega was captured and taken to the United States, where he was convicted on drug-trafficking charges. He is currently serving a forty-year sentence in a U.S. prison.

Liberty Returns

Shortly after General Noriega's arrest, Panama reestablished a civilian constitutional government. The Electoral Tribunal confirmed the May 1989 election of President Guillermo Endara. Endara completed his five-year term in 1994. His replacement was President Ernesto Pérez Balladares, who won an internationally monitored election with 33 percent of the vote. President Pérez Balladares successfully prepared Panama for the transfer of the Panama Canal to Panamanian sovereignty. He also oversaw major road construction projects.

In 1999 Mireya Elisa Moscoso Rodríguez was elected as the first female president of Panama. Her administration received high marks for social and educational programs for children. She also worked closely with the United States to combat drug trafficking and international terrorism. However, she failed to cut unemployment rates or to eliminate poverty, especially among blacks and the indigenous people. Environmentalists were especially critical of her decision to issue fishing licenses to Asian nations. The foreign fishing fleets are rapidly depleting Panama's marine treasures.

Panama's first female president was Mireya Elisa Moscoso Rodríguez.

Multiple-party democratic elections were held in May 2004. The newly elected president is Martín Torrijos Espino. Torrijos is the son of the former Panamanian dictator, Omar Torrijos Herrera. He drew especially strong support from the rural population and the urban poor. The new president has listed two major projects that he would like to accomplish early in his term. He would like to preside over a $5 billion expansion of the Panama Canal. President Torrijos is also interested in negotiating a new free-trade agreement with the United States.

Building a
Nation

HISTORICALLY, THE RESIDENTS OF PANAMA HAVE experienced many types of government. The Native Americans were led by tribal chiefs, a practice that survives today. During the Spanish colonial period the rulers of Spain appointed governors to administer the colony. Following independence from Spain, Panama was a province of New Granada and later of the Republic of Colombia. In 1903 Panama declared its independence and established a constitutional democracy. Since independence, the nation has suffered recurring instability, two military dictatorships, and continuing intervention by the United States.

The structure of the federal government in the Republic of Panama is determined by the constitution. The constitution calls for three separate branches of government: executive, legislative, and judicial. In Panama the executive branch is the most powerful branch of government.

Executive Leadership

The executive branch of government is made up of the president, first vice president, second vice president, and Cabinet of Ministers. The president and both vice

NATIONAL GOVERNMENT OF PANAMA

Executive Branch

PRESIDENT

FIRST VICE PRESIDENT

SECOND VICE PRESIDENT

CABINET OF MINISTERS

Legislative Branch

LEGISLATIVE ASSEMBLY (72 MEMBERS)

Judicial Branch

SUPREME COURT

SUPERIOR TRIBUNAL DISTRICT COURTS

CIRCUIT COURTS

MUNICIPAL COURTS

President Martín Torrijos Espino

Martín Torrijos Espino is the newly elected president of Panama. He attended Texas A&M University, where he majored in political science. He is young, handsome, and an excellent public speaker. Many Panamanians trust him to advocate for the poor and disadvantaged. He defeated his closest opponent by almost 20 percentage points.

presidents are elected to one five-year term by popular vote. Each candidate must be a native-born Panamanian whose age is thirty-five years or older. Candidates for president or vice president cannot run for reelection for ten years after completing their term in office. The power of the vice presidents is minimal. The first vice president is the chief executive when the president is absent. In addition, each vice president is allowed to vote during council meetings of the cabinet.

The real power is held by the president, who is also chief of state. The president has the authority to appoint and remove all cabinet ministers. The president is also responsible for maintaining public order, appointing a member of the Electoral Tribunal, and conducting foreign relations. If the president dies, resigns, or is removed from office, the first vice president assumes the presidency.

The cabinet ministers work very closely with the president. They help the country's leader to select provincial governors, prepare the budget, and negotiate contracts for

The National Flag

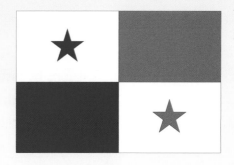

The national flag of Panama was designed by Manuel Amador, the son of Panama's first president, in October 1903. The flag is a rectangle with four equal-sized quarters. There are two white quadrants, one red quadrant, and one blue quadrant. White represents peace, and red and blue represent the major political parties at the time of independence. Red represents the Liberal Political Party, and blue represents the Conservative Political Party. The blue star in the upper-left quadrant stands for purity and honesty and the Conservative Party. The red star in the lower-right quadrant symbolizes authority and law and the Liberal Party. The flag was officially adopted by Law 64 on December 20, 1903.

government projects. They also advise the president on granting pardons to criminals.

Representatives of the People

The legislative branch of government is somewhat exceptional compared with other countries. It is a unicameral body (one house of representatives) rather than bicameral (two houses of representatives). In Panama there is only the Legislative Assembly, made up of seventy-two members. Members of the Legislative Assembly are elected to five-year terms in the same elections used to select the president and vice presidents. To be eligible for election, candidates must be at least twenty-five years old, and they must be Panamanian

Members of the Legislative Assembly meet here to create new laws, change old ones, and discuss treaties.

citizens by birth or naturalization. If they are naturalized citizens, they are required to have lived in Panama for at least fifteen years.

The Legislative Assembly has the power to write new laws, to modify or repeal old laws, and to ratify treaties. It can also declare war, grant amnesty for political offenses, and raise taxes. The constitution grants it the power to approve government contracts and the national budget. In the past, the Legislative Assembly seldom flexed its political muscles, and usually followed the lead of the executive branch. The new assembly appears to be leaning toward supporting the policies of President-elect Martín Torrijos. Torrijos's Democratic Revolutionary Party controls twenty-nine seats in the Assembly.

The constitution provides for the establishment of a separate government agency to administer elections and to guarantee that they are fair. This agency is known as the Electoral Tribunal and is made up of three members. Each of the three branches of government (executive, legislative, judicial) selects one member of the tribunal. The responsibilities of the Electoral Tribunal include overseeing voter registration, conducting elections, certifying election results, and judging charges that election laws have been violated. In Panama, every citizen over the age of eighteen is required to vote. There is no record, however, of nonvoters being punished by government officials.

Kuna Indians cast their ballots during the 2004 presidential elections.

EL VOTO SECRETO

EL VOT ES SECR

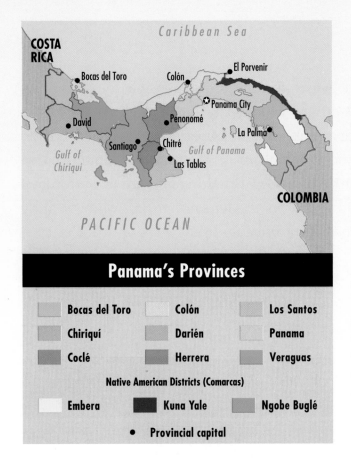

Panama's Provinces

▢ Bocas del Toro	▢ Colón	▢ Los Santos
▢ Chiriquí	▢ Darién	▢ Panama
▢ Coclé	▢ Herrera	▢ Veraguas

Native American Districts (Comarcas)

▢ Embera	▢ Kuna Yale	▢ Ngobe Buglé

● Provincial capital

Panama's Political Divisions

Provinces (9)	Capital	Population
Bocas del Toro	Bocas del Toro	89,269
Chiriquí	David	368,790
Coclé	Penonomé	202,461
Colón	Colón	204,208
Darién	La Palma	40,284
Herrera	Chitré	102,465
Los Santos	Las Tablas	83,495
Panama	Panama City	1,385,052
Veraguas	Santiago	209,076

Autonomous Native Districts (3)

Comarca Embera	No Capital	8,246
Comarca Kuna Yale	No Capital	32,446
Comarca Ngobe Buglé	No Capital	110,080

Administering the Law

The judicial branch of government is represented by a series of courts. The highest court in the land is the Supreme Court. It is composed of nine judges who are appointed to ten-year terms by the president. Two judges are replaced every two years. To serve on the Supreme Court, judges must be at least thirty-five years old and Panamanian by birth. They must also have a university law degree and either have taught or practiced law for a minimum of ten years.

The Supreme Court officially names thirty-six judges to five Superior Tribunal District Courts. The Superior Tribunal

District Court judges, in turn, are responsible for appointing the Circuit Court and Municipal Court judges. At the lowest court level, mayors choose administrative judges to handle minor civil and criminal cases. Most of the administrative judges have little or no legal training and are not attorneys. They frequently send poor defendants to jail while wealthy defendants pay fines or bribes.

Military Strength

After twenty-one years of military domination, the people of Panama decided to eliminate the military forces through their

Panama's police force keeps the peace at a workers strike.

elected representatives. They replaced the military with the Panamanian Public Forces, which consist of four independent units. The Panamanian National Police, the National Maritime Service, and the National Air Service are all responsible for law enforcement. The Institutional Protection Service provides security for important government guests.

All of these organizations are administered by civilians. Their budget is on public record and is controlled by the executive branch of the government. The elimination of the military forces in Panama has reduced the threat of an illegal military overthrow of an elected government.

Foreign Relations

Panama is an active member of the international and regional community. Panama has served a significant role in the United Nations as a full member of the General Assembly. The country has distinguished itself by serving responsibly for three terms on the U.N. Security Council. Panama is a member of the World Bank, the Inter-American Development Bank, and the International Monetary Fund.

On a regional perspective, Panama is a member of the Organization of American States and the Rio Group. The country helped establish the Union of Banana Exporting Countries and belongs to the Inter-American Tropical Tuna Commission. In 1994 Panama joined its Central American neighbors in signing the Alliance for Sustainable Development.

Panama City

Panama City was founded in 1519 by the Spanish governor of Panama, Pedro Arias Dávila. The city was the first significant European settlement on the western coast of the Americas. Today, the city can be viewed as three distinct locations. Old Panama, or Panamá Viejo, lies in ruins, the victim of a disastrous raid by Henry Morgan and his band of pirates. Colonial Panama—Casco Viejo, or Casco Antiguo—was built three years after the raid at a more defendable site. It contains the National Theater, the Cathedral, and the Church of San José with its famous gold-plated altar. Modern Panama City contains the financial district, luxury hotels, casinos, chic boutiques, and expensive restaurants. The whole city is an ethnic melting pot of Spanish descendents, black Caribbean islanders, Chinese, Lebanese, Mestizo, Native Americans, and many others. Almost one-third of all Panamanians live in the Panama City urban area. Daily temperatures are warm the entire year, with average January temperatures of 83°F (28.3°C) and July averages of 82°F (27.7°C). The average annual rainfall is 76 inches (193 cm), and is concentrated from May through November.

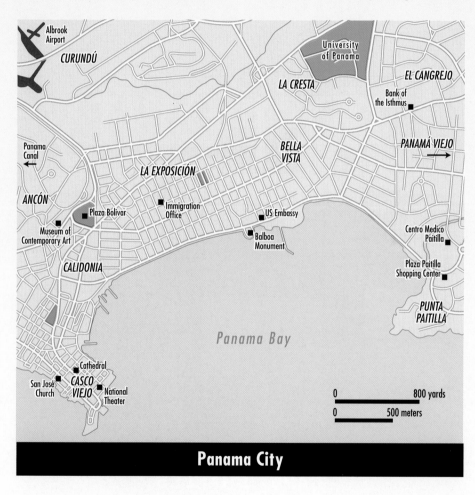

Panama City

In Search of Prosperity

CAPE CHARLES

PANAMA

H ISTORICALLY, PANAMA'S ECONOMY HAS BEEN CLOSELY tied to the United States. Since independence in 1903, the country has used the U.S. dollar as its paper currency. The United States has been Panama's major trade partner for both exports and imports. The successful construction and operation of the Panama Canal was associated with the United States. In recent years, however, Panama has developed a more international and diversified economic plan. Today, Panama's economy is dominated by a well-developed services sector. These services include banking, tourism, the Colón Free Trade Zone, transportation, and ship registration. Traditional sources of revenue like agriculture, mining, and manufacturing are now small contributors to the total economy.

Opposite: **Importing and exporting contribute to Panama's economic health. Here a large container ship passes through the Panama Canal.**

Panama is a leader in Latin America's banking sector. Panama City's financial district employs almost 13,000 people.

Show Me the Money

Panama has become Latin America's most important center for international banking. There are eighty-three different banks with total deposits of $27.3 billion operating in Panama. Fifty-three foreign banks from twenty-five nations have invested in the Panamanian banking sector. Almost 13,000 employees work in gleaming skyscrapers in Panama City's elegant financial district.

Panama's financial services sector has benefited from income from the Panama Canal. Ships passing through the Canal pay their crossing fees and purchase their supplies in Panama. Both foreign and domestic banks benefit from large international cash flows. The banks also benefit from Panama's use of U.S. dollars as paper currency. In Panama, interest rates, inflation, and exchange rates are closely tied to the United States. This has made investors feel more secure when they conduct business in Panama.

New laws passed in 1970 helped the financial sector expand dramatically. These laws provided absolute secrecy for international investors using Panamanian banks. The legislation also granted tax exemptions for investors operating outside of Panama. Many foreign investors moved their money to Panama because the laws protected their privacy.

Balboas and Dollars

The national currency of Panama is the balboa, although the country uses the United States dollar for its paper currency. The paper bills are identical to those used in the United States; Panama simply calls them balboas. Panama is the only country in the world whose constitution prohibits it from printing paper money. Panama mints its own coins, though, which it calls centavos. One hundred centavos equals one balboa or dollar. Centavos are the same size, value, and metal as U.S. coins. U.S. coins are also used and accepted in Panama.

However, there was a dark side to the secrecy involved in protecting them. Some of these clients were involved in illegal activities. Drug dealers used the banks to launder their profits from drug sales. Tax evaders, illegal weapons dealers, terrorists, and corrupt government officials from other countries also used the banks to hide money and avoid scrutiny.

Even though most of Panama's banking customers were honest, the country decided to protect its reputation by taking corrective action. Panama signed the Mutual Legal Assistance Treaty, which allowed inspectors to audit accounts suspected of illegal activities. The government also passed legislation that made money laundering a crime and increased penalties for drug trafficking.

Paradise Found

Political instability and more than thirty years of military dictatorships had a very negative impact on tourism. In 1989, when democracy was restored, the government immediately turned its attention to developing a tourism industry. The Institute for Panama Tourism was established. In 1993 the institute presented a new ten-year plan to the government. The plan focused on providing incentives to private investors who would help develop the tourism infrastructure. It outlined the need for construction of new hotels, roads, restaurants, and resorts. Programs to train managers and workers who would provide services to anticipated tourists were encouraged. The government accepted the plan and launched a broadly based campaign to attract investors.

Tourism is a growing industry in Panama. Here, a group of visitors explore the Darién jungle.

Ten years later the program had achieved unimagined success. More than 500,000 tourists visit Panama each year. Income earned from tourism was the second major source of foreign money, and thousands of new jobs were created. Many tourists returned to their homes exclaiming in delight about the natural beauty and laid back atmosphere to be found in Panama.

Panama's major tourist attractions include historic Spanish colonial ruins in Panama City, San Lorenzo, and Portobelo. Fourteen national parks provide unlimited opportunities for bird-watching and encounters with rare plants and animals. Sandy tropical islands near coral reefs provide superb snorkeling and scuba diving. A visit to the Panama Canal and a ride on the newly restored Panama Railroad offer exciting experiences.

The Big Ditch

The Panama Canal is truly one of the greatest engineering accomplishments in history. The canal, which is 50 miles (80.5 km) long, achieved a centuries-old dream by connecting the Atlantic and the Caribbean to the Pacific Ocean. After the French failed in their attempt to build the canal, President Theodore Roosevelt led the American effort to complete the gigantic task. U.S. engineers and more than 75,000 workers from around the world toiled for ten years on the project. The Panama Canal opened for traffic in 1914.

The United States operated the canal until December 31, 1999, when it turned the entire operation back to the people of Panama. Panama has done an excellent job of managing the canal. They have widened the Culebra (now called Gaillard) Cut to accommodate the passage of two ships at the same time. They are constructing a new bridge across the canal and are using satellites to manage canal traffic. Several facilities have been modernized to increase the efficiency of operations. Under Panamanian management, the time necessary for a ship to pass through the canal has been shortened. In addition, the number of accidents has been reduced significantly. Today, 9,000 workers are employed in canal operations. Approximately 14,000 ships pass through the canal each year at an average cost of $50,000 each. These fees are an important source of revenue for the economy of Panama.

As of late 1999, Panama has controlled canal operations, including the building of new bridges and managing canal traffic.

In 1855 the completion of the Panama Railroad marked the first transcontinental rail connection anywhere. The railroad served an important historic role in the migration of immigrants to California during the later years of the gold rush, which started in 1849. Later the railroad filled a critical role in the construction of the Panama Canal. It was used to move millions of tons of rock and soil. The railroad had fallen into disrepair by the 1990s, however, and was of little value to Panama.

In January 1998, the Panamanian government approved a contract to construct a new railroad along the old rail line. The contract called for the government of Panama to receive a percentage of all profits generated by the new railroad. The new line was completed in 2001 at a cost of $60 million. The railroad was designed primarily to haul containers across the isthmus. Passenger service is also available. Many Colón Free Zone executives commute by train between Colón and Panama City. Tourists are also taking advantage of the passenger service to enjoy a trip through rain forests and to view the Panama Canal.

These new locomotives are used for cargo as well as passenger service.

Let's Go Shopping

In 1944 the government of Panama created the Colón Free Trade Zone. The zone occupies 988 acres (400 ha) at the entrance of the Panama Canal near the city of Colón. It is the largest free trade zone in the Western Hemisphere and the second largest in the world.

More than $11 billion worth of exports and imports move through the zone each year. This activity generates almost $1 billion of income for Panama. With more than 2,000 companies operating in the Colón Free Trade Zone, an average of 250,000 businesspeople and tourists arrive each year.

Ship Registrations

The country of Panama earns more than $50 million each year by registering ships. Every ship that travels in international waters is required to be officially registered. Panama began registering ships in 1925. Today it is number one in the world in both the number of ships and the tonnage it registers. Approximately 21 percent of the world's merchant fleet flies the flag of Panama, though most of the ships registered in Panama are owned by Japanese and Greek shipping companies.

Most foreign owners register their ships in Panama to save money. Panama gives discounts on the registration fees and charges less for taxes than other nations do. Panama also

System of Weights and Measures

Panama uses both the metric and the imperial systems of weights and measures. Distances are given in both kilometers and miles.

Panama has one of the oldest and largest ship registries. The number of ships registered to Panama has grown so large that it has become the top fleet in the world.

gives ship owners the opportunity to avoid labor and wage regulations they would have to follow in their own countries. Another attraction for owners is the lack of enforcement of strict safety and security rules in Panama. Most owners are honest businessmen, but some owners operating unsafe ships take advantage of the loose rules in Panama.

Industrial Activity

Historically, industrial development in Panama has been very weak. Even now manufacturing generates less than 15 percent of the nation's income. Most of Panama's factories are engaged in food and beverage processing for local consumption. There is also a number of small factories producing textiles and clothing. More than 60 percent of all industrial production is concentrated in Panama City.

Madden Dam was built in 1935 to control the waters of the Chagres River. Today, one of its primary functions is to produce hydro-electric power.

One bright light shining in Panama's industrial sector is the production of electricity. Panama generates slightly over 50 percent of its electrical needs from waterpower. Large amounts of rainfall and steep valleys have created a good natural environment for hydro-electric generation. Hydro-electricity is an excellent source of power because it is clean and renewable.

What Panama Grows, Makes, and Mines

Agriculture (2000 est.)

Sugarcane	2,000,000 metric tons
Bananas	807,400 metric tons
Rice	319,100 metric tons

Manufacturing (1998 est.)

Raw sugar	166,000 metric tons
Processed milk	39,300 metric tons
Salt	22,500 metric tons

Mining

Mining data is considered private information, and production figures are not released.

Cerro Punta is a large agricultural area due to its fertile soil.

Tilling the Soil

Most of the Panamanians engaged in farming are very poor. They have small farms, and the soils of Panama are not high in quality. They raise subsistence crops of corn, beans, and rice—that is, most of their crop is used to feed their families, leaving little surplus to sell for cash. An exception to this pattern can be found in the rich volcanic soils of the western highlands. In the valley of the Río Cerro Punta near Costa Rica, vegetables, fruit, and coffee are grown in abundance.

Today many non-Panamanian companies own banana fields in Panama. Here, bananas are being harvested by an employee of the Chiquita Company.

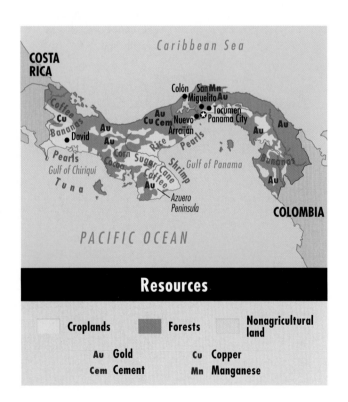

COSTA RICA

Caribbean Sea

Colón San Mn
Miguelito Au
Au Tocumen
Cu Cem Panama City
Nuevo
Arraiján Pearls

Coffee
Cu
Bananas
David Au
Au
Corn
Pearls Cocoa Sugar
Gulf of Chiriquí Cane Shrimp
Coffee Gulf of Panama
Tuna Au

Rice

Au

Bananas

Au

Azuero
Peninsula

COLOMBIA

PACIFIC OCEAN

Resources

Croplands   Forests   Nonagricultural land

Au Gold   Cu Copper
Cem Cement   Mn Manganese

There are some large commercial farms owned by wealthy landowners. They raise crops such as bananas, sugarcane, rice, and coffee. Vast plots of sugarcane are harvested on the Azuero Peninsula. Bananas are Panama's number one agricultural export. They have been an important crop since the 1890s. Minor C. Keith, an American investor, started the banana industry when he bought large blocks of land near Colón. He became extremely wealthy when he helped form the United Fruit Company in 1899. At that time, the United Fruit Company was the largest agricultural company in the world. Most profits from banana production have gone to foreign owners and do not help Panama's economy as much as they should.

Harvesting the Sea

For many years, the export of shrimp has generated important revenue for Panama. There are more than 200 shrimp trawling vessels in Panama. Most of the shrimp are harvested in the shallow bays along the Pacific coastline. In addition, Panama has some of the most developed commercial shrimp farms in the world. In 2000 a disease called white-spot virus almost wiped out the shrimp population. Chronic disease and excess harvesting could damage the long-term prospects of the shrimping industry.

In Search of Wealth

Panama has not been blessed with many mineral resources. The export of mining products is almost nonexistent, although Panama claims to have the largest gold mine in Central America. Production figures, however, are protected and unreliable. There are some very high-grade reserves of copper in Panama. Most of the copper is located on land belonging to indigenous people, who are opposed to mining on their lands. Environmentalists have come to their support to protect their natural surroundings. Panama's future economy will not be centered on mining activities. The most likely area of growth will occur in the tourist sector.

The Melting Pot

84

P ANAMA'S POPULATION HAS REACHED THE 3,120,000 MARK according to the most recent population estimate (2002). This is a significant number, if one considers that the country's total population was 600,000 only seventy years ago. The numbers have been increasing rapidly because improved health care has cut the death rate, while the birth rate has remained moderately high. It is also a young population, with almost one-third of Panamanians under fifteen years of age.

Opposite: **Panama's diverse population has grown to over 3 million people.**

Where Are the People?

The population of Panama is not evenly distributed across the country. There are areas where very few people live and other areas with high population density. More than 50 percent of all Panamanians live in the corridor connecting Panama City with Colón along the Panama Canal. The densest concentration lies in the urban area surrounding Panama City. This urban region contains one-third of the nation's citizens. Many people move to Panama City (rural to urban migration) in search of jobs, better health care, and better educational opportunities.

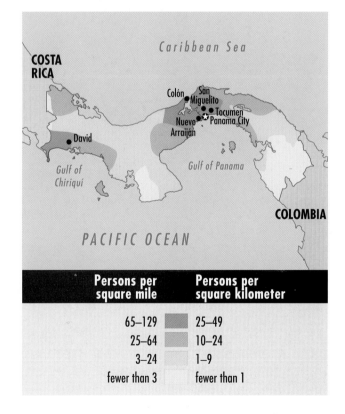

Persons per square mile	Persons per square kilometer
65–129	25–49
25–64	10–24
3–24	1–9
fewer than 3	fewer than 1

Street scene in Chiriquí Province

Chiriquí Province is the second largest province in both size and population. Located in the southwestern portion of Panama, most of the people are found in towns along the Pan-American Highway. The hills and lowlands of central Panama west of the canal contain the third pocket of significant population density. This region is the heartland of Panama's rural population. Surrounded by ranches and farms, the cities of Penonomé, Santiago, Chitré, and Las Tablas are important market towns and provincial capitals.

East of Panama City and Colón, the number of inhabitants decreases dramatically. Darién Province has vast areas of tropical rain forest where there are no permanent residents. Swamps, almost impenetrable jungle, poisonous snakes, swarming insects, and dangerous drug traffickers make this a place that many people choose to avoid. There is a second population void along the Caribbean coast. The city of Colón represents the only significant pocket of population. The remaining coastal region contains only 5 percent of the total population.

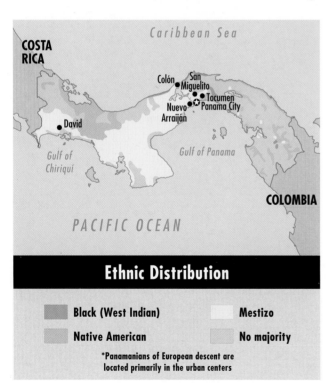

Ethnic Distribution

Black (West Indian)   Mestizo

Native American   No majority

*Panamanians of European descent are located primarily in the urban centers

Ethnic Diversity

Panama is a true "melting pot" of ethnic variety. The Spanish came to establish a colonial empire and found a thriving Native American culture. Chinese originally came to build the Panama Railroad. Other foreign ethnic groups arrived during the construction of the Panama Canal, especially blacks from the Caribbean Basin. Lebanese businessmen arrived to escape a civil war in Lebanon. Indians and Pakistanis came in search of commercial opportunities. Visitors to Panama City will recognize the faces of many nationalities and hear a wide assortment of languages.

Mestizos are the largest ethnic group in Panama, comprising 70 percent of the population. They are a mixture of Spanish and Native American blood. Mestizos are found in many layers of Panamanian life. Some are successful upper-class professionals—doctors and lawyers—and politicians. Others are middle-class businesspeople, teachers, health care workers, and canal employees. The largest segment of the mestizo population is bound to subsistence farming or life in urban slums with high unemployment and poverty.

Ethnic Breakdown

Mestizo (Spanish and Native American)	70%
Black (West Indian)	14%
European (Mostly Spanish)	10%
Native American	6%

A mestiza girl celebrates at the Corpus Christi festival.

Panama's black population is the second largest ethnic group with 14 percent of the total population. Most of Panama's black population originated in the West Indies islands of the Caribbean Sea. Blacks were heavily recruited to work on the Panama Canal. The French recruited black laborers primarily from Jamaica. Thousands of Jamaican blacks died while working for the French. So, when the United States started work on the canal, the Jamaican government prohibited it from recruiting workers from Jamaica. As a result, the United States recruited large numbers of blacks from the island of Barbados. Several thousand blacks were also taken to Panama to work on the banana plantations.

The black population of Panama has suffered substantial racial discrimination. The Hispanic and mestizo population maintained a long-lived hostility toward blacks. The blacks were seen to be different. They spoke English instead of Spanish. They were Protestants instead of Roman Catholics. They were dark-skinned, and their cultural traditions were more African than European. Most

The black population is the second largest in Panama.

Panamanian blacks today have lived under lower-class economic opportunities. Many struggled for years without electricity, running water, or proper sewage disposal. Their unemployment rates have always been high compared with other ethnic groups. In the 1941 constitution, blacks were even deprived of their Panamanian citizenship as an open act of racism. Although citizenship was restored to them in 1946, racial discrimination against blacks is still occurring in Panama today.

Approximately 10 percent of Panamanians claim pure European bloodlines. Most are descendants of the original Spanish colonists. They are very protective of their ethnic purity, and many refuse to marry outside their ethnic circle of friends. They are proud of their light-colored skin and occasional blond hair and green eyes. Almost all of this group live in the best urban residential neighborhoods, especially in Panama City. This elite group controls much of Panama's wealth, and many occupy high-level government positions. They lost control of the government to the mestizo and black populations during the Torrijos and Noriega dictatorships, but they are back in power again.

The First Inhabitants

When the Spanish arrived in Panama in 1501, an estimated sixty different Native American tribes lived on the isthmus. Today, there are only six tribes remaining. The Kuna, Emberá, and Wounaan (Choco) are found in Darién Province and the San Blas Islands. The Ngobe-Buglé (Guaymí) live mostly in

Population of Panama's Cities (2004 est.)	
Panama City	463,093
San Miguelito	314,000
Colón	175,000
David	125,000
Tocumen	90,000
Arraiján	69,100
La Chorrera	59,900
Pacora	59,400

An Emberá woman and her handmade baskets

Chiriquí, Veraguas, and Bocas del Toro provinces. The Teribe and Bókatá are found in Bocas del Toro. Currently, pure-blooded Native Americans make up only about 6 percent of Panama's population. Large numbers of Native Americans died long ago from European diseases. Thousands more perished at the hands of the Spanish conquistadors or from the harsh labor conditions during forced slavery.

The government of Panama has been trying to increase its protection of the Native American people. They have established three political units, called comarcas—like reservations—where the indigenous people make most of the decisions that affect their lives. The constitution now protects their ethnic identity and language. The government requires bilingual education programs in these Native American communities. The Federal Family Code recognizes that traditional marriage rites are equal to Panamanian civil marriage ceremonies.

Kuna Indians

The Kuna Indians, numbering approximately 30,000, live primarily on the San Blas Islands and the coast of Darién Province. They live a contented life without many of the complexities of Western societies. Mothers are at the top of the power structure, and inheritance is determined by the women and not the men. Young men are required to live in their mother-in-law's house after they marry and to work with their fathers-in-law. The Kuna seldom divorce, but if they do, it is a simple task. The husband packs his clothes and leaves the house and the marriage is over.

Families divide household responsibilities and required tasks. Men harvest coconuts, grow food crops, fish, cut firewood, make house repairs, sew their own and their sons' clothing, and weave baskets. Women cook, collect freshwater, sew female clothing, do the laundry, and clean the house. The birth of a daughter is a prized event. Women dress much more spectacularly than men. Kuna women wear gold nose rings, arm and leg bands, and beautiful blouses with elaborate designs called *molas*.

Increasing numbers of tourists descend upon the Kuna each year. While the visits generate needed cash income for the families, such exposure to Western culture is a very real threat to their traditional society.

There are an estimated 100,000 East and South Asians living in Panama. The most populous of these groups are the ethnic Chinese. Their ancestors were taken to Panama to help build the Panama Railroad. Many of them died of malaria and yellow fever. A mass suicide claimed the lives of many other Chinese railroad workers when supervisors banned their use of opium, a cultural tradition. Some Chinese moved to California when the railroad was completed. A significant number, however, remained and established Chinatown in Panama City. Here, tourists can shop in Chinese grocery stores, eat ethnic Chinese foods, and purchase fine silks in general stores.

Panamanian Chinese celebrate Chinese New Year in Panama City's Chinatown.

A Multilingual Nation

There are very few countries where visitors will have the opportunity to hear as many different languages as in Panama. The owner of a Greek restaurant might call out instructions to his staff in traditional Greek. An Indian merchant in Colón chats in Urdu with his neighbor. A Lebanese jeweler says his prayers in Arabic at the community mosque. Mandarin Chinese echoes through the aisles of a Chinese grocery store.

While many international languages are heard in Panama, the official language is Spanish. Approximately 85 percent of all Panamanians speak Spanish as their first language. Another 14 percent speak English as their first language. Most Caribbean blacks are native English speakers since they originally came from Jamaica and Barbados, which were British colonies. The government of Panama is encouraging its citizens to become bilingual in Spanish and English. The rapid growth of the tourist industry requires that more workers become fluent in English. The banking sector also employs large numbers of English-speaking workers.

A sign in Spanish and English supports Panama's belief in a dual language country.

Common Spanish words and phrases:

Adiós.	Good bye.
Buenos días.	Good morning.
Buenas noches.	Good night/evening.
Como está usted?	How are you?
Cuánto?	How much?
Dónde está?	Where is ...?
Habla usted español?	Do you speak Spanish?
Gracias.	Thank you.
Por favor.	Please.
Qué hora es?	What time is it?

Time to Study

The people of Panama are very serious about their educational goals. They are developing many programs to ensure that all of the country's citizens can read and write. The government currently spends almost 20 percent of its annual budget on education. All education in Panama is free up to the university level. Substantial progress has resulted from this determined, widely supported effort. There is a 92.6 percent literacy rate in Panama today.

One method used to guarantee success was the passage of legislation requiring all Panamanian children to complete the sixth grade. Currently, 95 percent of Panama's children attend primary school (grades 1 through 6). Failure to attend school usually occurs in remote areas where there is a lack of transportation or where parents feel that education is not important. Throughout Panama, only 62 percent of children attend secondary schools. The Ministry of Education is now working diligently to expand opportunities for secondary education.

Panama's bustling service economy requires increasingly large numbers of university graduates. The leading institutions of higher education are the University of Panama, the Technological University, and the University of Santa María La Antigua. Nearly 100,000 students are enrolled in university educational programs. University students are also social activists. They demonstrate for political and social change and sometimes come into violent conflict with authorities. University students were foremost leaders in demanding the return of the Panama Canal to Panama.

It is a requirement for all Panamanian children to attend school through sixth grade.

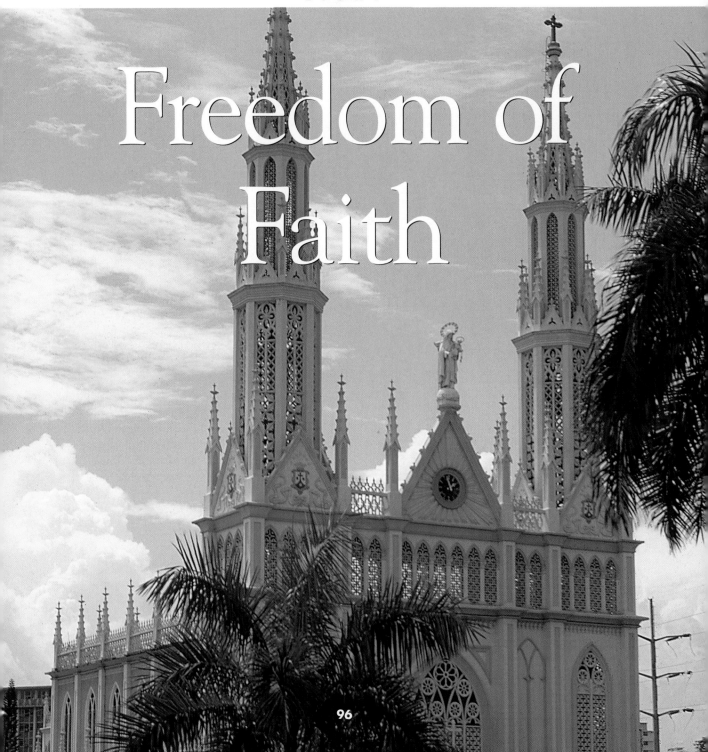

Freedom of Faith

P

ANAMA'S CONSTITUTION GUARANTEES THAT THERE SHALL be no prejudice with respect to religious freedom. People of all religious beliefs are free to practice their faith in Panama as long as Christian morality and public order are respected. Because Panama's citizens represent a variety of different cultural and ethnic groups, many different religions are practiced.

Opposite: **Panama City Cathedral**

Roman Catholics

The nation's constitution recognizes that Roman Catholicism is the religion of the majority of Panamanians. The constitution, however, does not designate the Roman Catholic Church as the official state religion. The constitution does require that Catholicism be taught in the public schools. Parents may request that their children not attend religion classes.

Historically, the organization of the Roman Catholic Church in Panama has been weak. One of the biggest problems today is a shortage of priests. Almost every town in Panama has a Catholic church, but many of these churches do not have a resident priest. This is especially true in the more remote areas of the country where a priest may visit the congregation only a few times each year. In 2001 there were fewer than 400 priests serving all of Panama. A significant percentage of them were foreigners.

Attendance at Catholic churches is highest in the urban congregations and sparse in many rural areas. However, no

Major Religions

Roman Catholic	82%
Protestant, including Evangelicals	15%
Other religions	3%

Sunday Mass is well attended at El Carmen Church in Panama City.

Women in Panama play a large role in church activities. Here, a woman arranges flowers on the altar at the Don Bosco Basilica in Panama City.

matter how devout a Panamanian Catholic is, participation in the sacraments is considered essential. The first sacrament is baptism. Baptism symbolizes a child's entry into society and the church community. Even in rural areas, families will travel great distances for a baptismal ceremony. The second most significant sacrament is first communion. The last essential sacrament is the receiving of the last rites to prepare an individual for eternity. There may be extended lapses of time between these sacraments, when many Panamanians do not actively practice their religion at all. This is particularly true of men.

Catholic churches in rural areas and smaller towns are dominated by women. After boys reach manhood, many drift away from active participation at church. Although they still consider themselves Catholics, they may attend church only for weddings or at Christmas and Easter. Girls, on the other hand, are active in the church throughout their lives. They attend Mass regularly and support church-sponsored activities. For many women, church activities fulfill two strong elements in their lives. The first is spiritual, and the second is social.

The Church of San José

One of Panama's most famous religious sites is the Church of San José. The church was originally located in Panama Viejo. It was one of very few buildings to survive the sacking of Panama City by the notorious pirate Henry Morgan in 1671. Most of the city's buildings were burned to the ground. The Church of San José, with its magnificent, hand-carved wooden altar, survived. Devout Catholics believed that God protected the church and that its survival was a "true miracle."

When Panama City was rebuilt at its present location, a new Church of San José was constructed. The famous wooden altar was taken from Panama Viejo and installed in the new church. To protect the wood from decay, the entire altar was covered in gold leaf. Today, Panamanians have nicknamed the church the "Church of the Gold Altar." It is located near the historic seawall and has become one of Panama City's most popular tourist destinations.

All Soul's Day

One of the most significant Catholic religious holidays in Panama is All Soul's Day on November 2. This is an especially important holy day among rural Panamanians. Even though they may not be active in church events, they possess a strong belief in the reward or punishment of Judgment Day. Many believe that on All Soul's Day everyone who died during the previous year is called before God and the devil for judgment. At this time, Saint Peter reads the life record of the individual. The good and bad deeds are weighed on a Roman balance scale. If good deeds outweigh the bad, the individual will enter heaven for eternity. If the scale tips in favor of the bad deeds, the person will accompany the devil to hell for eternity.

The Church of the Black Christ

The statue of the Black Christ

One of the most interesting legends in Panama's religious history is connected to an image of Jesus Christ. The life-size figure of Jesus is known as the Cristo Negro de Portobelo—the Black Christ of Portobelo. The statue, which is carved of dark wood, is encased in a permanent display in the Church of San Felipe, which was dedicated in 1814.

There is no documented historical evidence of how the statue happened to arrive in Portobelo. Some legends state that it originated in Spain and was being shipped to Colombia. Others say it was carved from local wood and was destined for Spain. Regardless of its true origin, the statue has been in Portobelo since the seventeenth century and is believed to have the power to create miracles.

Pilgrims show their devotion to the Black Christ by crawling on their knees.

In the early 1800s the image of the Black Christ gained new fame. The Isthmus of Panama was being ravaged by a cholera epidemic. Portobelo's citizens prayed to the image of the Black Christ to spare them from this deadly disease. They promised that if they were spared, they would celebrate with a special feast day in honor of the Black Christ. The epidemic bypassed the city.

Since that time, every October 21, religious pilgrims gather in Portobelo to celebrate the Feast of the Black Christ. More than 60,000 pilgrims from Latin America, the Caribbean Basin, Europe, and the United States arrive each year for the celebration. Some Panamanians walk as many as 124 miles (200 km) as penance for their sins. Some pilgrims fall into a religious trance and crawl on their knees the last portion of the journey. They arrive with serious cuts and bleeding knees, seemingly unaware of any pain.

The celebration is a mixture of religious and pagan rites. Thousands of participants arrive several days early. The small town's streets are packed with people participating in a Mardi

Thousands of people hold candles during the annual Black Christ festival in Portobelo.

Gras type of event. Alcohol flows freely, with more rum and beer sold in a week than during the rest of the year. Gambling occurs all over the town with dice, card games, and roulette. Illegal cockfights are held in dimly lit alleys.

At eight o'clock on October 21 all activity ceases. The pilgrims line the streets with lighted candles. The doors of the Church of San Felipe are thrown open. The image of the Black Christ is put on a platform and carried on the shoulders of eighty devotees as it passes through the streets. For this special occasion, the statue is covered with a scarlet robe trimmed in gold. Some believers pin pictures of missing loved ones on the robe. Others attach photos of sick or injured family members and friends to the cloth with notes praying for help. Some even pin lottery tickets to the robe in hopes of gaining new wealth.

For four hours, the image slowly moves through the streets. Even though it is the rainy season, believers claim it never rains during the parade. Legend claims that the statue refuses to be taken back to the church before midnight. Finally it is time for the image to be returned to the church. The doors close, and the partying erupts once again and continues until dawn. The next day the pilgrims depart, and Portobelo settles back into the patterns of a small, quiet fishing village.

Protestants

There are several active Protestant church denominations in Panama. Some groups are the Baptists, Lutherans, Episcopalians, Methodists, and Presbyterians. The Caribbean blacks are the principal members of the non-Catholic churches. Their membership is concentrated in Panama City and Colón.

The weak organization of the Roman Catholic Church has encouraged a strong Evangelical movement in Panama. The Evangelicals are members of major Protestant denominations but view themselves as different. They stress that they are born-again Christians, and have a deep commitment to share their religious beliefs with others. As a result, they are active in missionary programs whose goals focus on helping others to find a spiritual rebirth into a life dedicated to God.

The Evangelicals may represent as many as two-thirds of all Protestants. They recruit new members largely from the lower socioeconomic classes and the indigenous peoples. In their work with the indigenous, they give away copies of the New Testament of the Bible in all six indigenous languages. The Evangelicals have also been active in building schools on the comarcas, where they provide religious training as well as regular classes.

One of the fastest growing religious groups in Panama is the Church of Jesus Christ of Latter-Day Saints (Mormons). The church has over thirty thousand members and not long ago built its first temple in Panama City. Most of the growth is the result of the work of more than 200 active missionaries. The Mormon missionaries are young adults who have recently graduated from high schools in the United States. Many of these young people go door-to-door, working up to sixteen hours a day, six days a week, in an attempt to recruit new members.

Other Faiths

Panama's location at the crossroads of the world's two major oceans has attracted immigrants from across the globe. Many of these immigrants have taken the faiths of their ancestors with them. In addition to Christian churches, Panama has Muslim mosques, Jewish synagogues, a Hindu temple, and a Baha'i house of worship. The Muslim community is the largest with more than 140,000 members. Traditional Chinese religions are also practiced.

The Jewish community in Panama is small (7,000) but very influential. Most of the Jewish community is composed of wealthy businessmen and their families who live in Panama City, Colón, and David. In Panama City, there are two Jewish high schools, a Hebrew Cultural Center, and a Jewish Sports Club. Recently, 1,000 immigrants from Israel added significantly to the Jewish population. Panama is unique politically as regards the Jewish community. It is the only country in the world besides Israel that has elected two Jewish presidents in the twentieth century.

Although the Baha'i religion has a small following, Panama has one of only seven Baha'i houses of worship in the world. The House of Worship was completed in 1972 and was

Along with Catholicism, Islam is also practiced in Panama.

Offerings fill a Santería altar.

built to serve members from all of Central America. The temple is perched on a high cliff overlooking the Panama Canal. Members of all religious faiths are welcome to worship.

Religious Holidays in Panama	
Día de los Tres Reyes Magos (Three Kings' Day)	January 6
Ash Wednesday	March or April
Good Friday	March or April
Easter	March or April
All Souls' Day	November 2
Christmas	December 25

Santería

A small minority of Panamanians, mostly Caribbean blacks, practice a West African religion known as Santería, or the way of the saints. The religion arrived in Cuba with Yoruba slaves from Nigeria and Benin. The practice then spread from Cuba to the islands of the Caribbean and eventually to Panama.

Followers of Santería focus on *ashé*, which is the force that maintains order and balance in the universe. If something is out of balance in the life of an individual, he needs to contact a benevolent spirit (an *orisha*) for help. The Yoruba listed more than 1,700 spirits who could be contacted. In Panama, most followers of Santería limit their contact to fewer than two dozen spirits.

True believers of this religion communicate with the orishas through prayer, ritual, and sacrifices when they are seeking help. Sometimes ceremonies are held to seek power and wealth from an orisha. Requests may also be made to place a curse upon an enemy, or even to kill him. Sacrifices may include feasts, baths, cigar smoke, food offerings, and animal blood. If an animal is sacrificed, it must be treated with great respect, as all life and all death are sacred.

A Wealth of Culture

P ANAMA REPRESENTS A JIGSAW PUZZLE OF CULTURAL CHARacteristics. It serves as a link between South and Central American cultures. The Panama Canal has made it a crossroads and melting pot of world cultures. The country and its people reflect a cultural diversity seldom found in individual nations.

Panama is a lively country. The clothes are colorful, the food spicy and varied, and the music invigorating. The people are warm, generous, and fun-loving. Strangers are welcomed with open arms and included in local and national celebrations. The family remains the firm foundation of Panamanian society.

Opposite: **A procession of dancers at the Corpus Christi festival**

Home Is Where the Heart Is

Parents and grandparents are treated with deep respect in Panama. Children frequently choose to live close to home or with their parents until they marry. Birthdays, weddings, baptisms, and national holidays are celebrated within the family unit. The family is a source of great security. In times of difficulty and stress the family can always be counted on for support.

Family bonds are strong in Panama.

Marriage Customs

Many mestizo and black couples from lower economic classes do not legally marry. They engage in an informal marriage where both individuals consent to live together without a marriage license or official ceremony. Children from these consensual unions are not regarded as social outcasts. Their status in society is the same as children from legal marriages. Later in life, the husband and wife, encouraged by adult children, often partici-pate in a formal marriage ceremony. On other occa-sions, a local priest may suggest that the couple participate in an official church wedding. Wealthy ranchers and farmers, as well as urban middle class and elite pairs, participate in standard legal ceremonies. The elite believe that the marriage should ensure racial purity and guarantee access to wealth and property, reflecting widely held attitudes about class and status.

The tradition of making a scarecrow takes place at the end of every year in Panama.

Folklore

In the countryside, many rural peasants are superstitious. They believe in the power of *curanderos* (faith healers). They trust the curanderos to use prayer, herbal medicines, and secret rites and potions to heal their diseases. Some peasants believe in the existence of witches. To prevent a witch from causing harm, they think it is necessary to turn a piece of clothing inside out. Black cats and dogs may be evil demons and are a cause of fear. Wearing a necklace made of jaguar or crocodile teeth is believed to be the best way to drive off evil spirits.

At New Year, a special tradition is practiced in some parts of Panama. A scarecrowlike figure is made by stuffing a pair of men's pants and a shirt with straw. Frequently a round gourd head with a painted face is attached to the body. These figures are seated on chairs in front of houses a few days before New Year's Day. On December 31, when the clock strikes midnight, the straw man is set on fire. This action marks the passing of the old year and welcomes in the new year.

Music, the Soul of Panama

It is claimed by some that music flows through the veins of the Panamanian people. The lifeblood of Panamanian music is salsa. Salsa is a mixture of Afro-Cuban, Afro–Puerto Rican, and Latin-Caribbean traditional dance music mixed with rhythm and blues, jazz, and rock, often played at fast tempos. Salsa bands usually have eight to ten musicians and one or two lead singers. The instruments played to create the unique sounds of salsa include trombones, a piano, bass, timbales, a cowbell, congo drums, bongos, and other percussion instruments. The lively beat of salsa is heard on buses, street corner boom boxes, and in nightclubs. It pours from the doorways of private homes in the evenings. Salsa is a specialty of Panama, and Ruben Blades is its best-known performer.

Dancing Feet

The Panamanian love for music includes a passion for dancing. During holidays and on weekends the nightclubs are full of couples who perform the salsa and merengue (meringue) dances. The national dance of Panama is the *tamborito* (little drummer). It is a couple's dance in which the music is provided by drums and female vocals. The theme of the dance is an attempt by the man to court the female dancer and to win her affection.

The King of Salsa

Ruben Blades is one of the most recognized citizens of Panama. He possesses unlimited artistic talent. He is a brilliant composer, songwriter, and singer. He has recorded more than twenty albums and won four Grammy Awards. His song "Pedro Navaja" is the biggest selling single record in the history of salsa music. Ruben Blades is also an accomplished actor who has starred in movies with Robert Redford, Whoopi Goldberg, Richard Pryor, and Jack Nicholson.

Blades earned a master's degree in international law at Harvard Law School. He is a well-known political activist. Many of his songs contain lyrics that call for social change in Latin America. In 1994 he ran for president of Panama. He did very well, finishing third in the election with 18 percent of the total vote. His reputation as a socially responsible activist led to a prestigious appointment by the United Nations. In

1999 he was appointed as one of seven Goodwill Ambassadors for the World Conference Against Racism. In August 2004 Ruben Blades was named as Panama's new tourism czar by President-elect Martín Torrijos Espino.

The dancers wear elegant costumes that are an important part of this traditional folk dance. The women wear the *pollera*—an embroidered two-piece dress. The skirt is very full, and it is worn with several layers of petticoats. Satin slippers complete the costume. Many times the women adorn themselves with thousands of dollars worth of gold jewelry. The jewelry is often passed down from mother to daughter for several generations.

The male dancers wear ankle-length pants and sandals. Their shirts are called *montuños*. They are long shirts with a hanging fringe along the bottom. They also wear a traditional Panama hat called a *sombrero pintada* (painted hat). The music, costumes, and dance movements make the tamborito an elegant and romantic experience.

Congos are another popular folk dance performed during holidays and festivals, especially *Carnaval* (Carnival) held on Shrove Tuesday, introducing Lent. The congo dance originated among the African slaves taken to Panama by the Spanish. The slaves created the dance to make fun of the Spaniards and their traditions. During the dance the performers sing songs in dialects with many words of African origin. Since the Spaniards did not understand the language being spoken by the slaves, they were unaware that the dancers were ridiculing them.

Dancers perform the traditional congo.

Everybody loves to watch the congo dancers. The women wear brightly colored dresses with full skirts. They place large tropical flowers in their pulled-back hair. With drums beating and the crowd chanting, the women shake their hips to the fast rhythm.

The men, on the other hand, dress in tattered old clothes. They often use ropes for belts and fasten metal objects and doll heads on the ropes. Sometimes they circle the women dancers on all fours in an attempt to capture them. Somehow, the ladies always escape, to the delight of the spectators. The congos are joy-filled dances full of good humor and laughter.

Even though Panama is a small country, it has produced many excellent painters and writers. Roberto Lewis studied art in Paris and won prizes in several national and international exhibitions. Lewis taught painting at Panama's National Institute of Art for more than twenty-five years. The large murals he painted in the National Theater and Presidential Palace are Lewis's most popular legacy. Don Manuel Amador was a gifted oil painter who worked in landscapes and human figures. The son of a president, he also designed the national flag of Panama. Humberto Ivaldi is considered Panama's finest landscape painter because of his skillful uses of color and shading.

Roberto Lewis's mural of the explorer Balboa in Panama's Presidential Palace.

Ricardo Miró is recognized as the national poet of Panama. He held a deep affection for his country, and Panama was the topic of many of his poems. One of his most beautiful and popular poems is "Patricia" ("Mother Country"), written in 1909.

Currently, Enrique Jaramillo Levi is acknowledged to be Panama's leading writer. He has been successful in writing essays, poems, and books and editing anthologies. He is a master storyteller whose work has been published in seven languages. One of his recent contributions was the founding of *Magician*, a magazine that focuses on Panamanian culture.

Each year, the Panamanian Ministry of Commerce and Industry sponsors a National Fair of Crafts. Artisans from every corner of Panama display their handicrafts at the Atlantic and Pacific (ATLAPA) Convention Center in Panama City. Paintings, ceramics, leather products, wood and stone carvings, woven textiles, and indigenous crafts are represented at the fair. Judges present prizes to the winning artisan in each handicraft category. A large plaque and cash prize are awarded for the item that is selected as "The Craft of the Year."

The town of La Pintada is well-known for its sombrero pintada hats. These painted hats are a part of Panama's national costume for men. The province of Los Santos is the

Panama Canal Museum (Museo del Canal Interoceánico)

The Panama Canal Museum is housed in one of the most beautiful buildings in Panama. It is an elegant structure originally built as the Grand Hotel in 1875. The building was purchased by the French in 1881 to serve as headquarters while they attempted to build the Canal.

In 1910 the Panamanian government took over ownership of the building. When the United States agreed to return the Panama Canal to Panama, a decision was made to convert the building into a museum. The Panamanians lovingly restored the building with great pride and artistic skill. Today, the museum contains the world's best collection of artifacts, photographs, films, and videos related to the history of the Panama Canal.

Woman in a traditional pollera

main source of the beautiful hand-made polleras, the Panamanian national dress for women. The towns of Chitré and Las Tablas are noted for their fine pottery.

The most popular handicrafts in Panama are produced by the indigenous people. The all-time favorites are the cotton molas created by the Kuna tribe. Molas generally have from two to seven layers of brightly colored cloth panels fashioned in a specific design. Geometric figures and rain forest plants and animals are common designs. Red, black, and orange are favorite colors, and the dyes are exceptionally bright. The artist sketches a design on the top panel of cloth and cuts out the design pattern. On each of the under layers, the cut of the design is smaller so that each color is displayed

The handcrafted mola is designed and created by members of the Kuna tribe.

in the final product. The stitching is done by hand, and the finer the stitch, the more valuable the mola. Kuna women wear the beautiful molas on the front and back of their blouses.

The Wounaan and Emberá tribes of the Darién rain forest carve delicate figures from the *tagua* nut. The tagua nut is the seed produced by several species of tagua palm trees. The nut is commonly about the size of a chicken egg. It is referred to as vegetable ivory because it looks like the ivory in elephant and walrus tusks. A healthy female tagua palm will produce about 20 pounds (9 kilograms) of vegetable ivory each year. This amount of ivory is equal to an average female elephant tusk. The most common tagua carvings represent animals of the rain forest. The Emberá also carve spirit masks from tropical woods. These masks are believed to frighten off evil spirits that cause illness.

Baskets of the Emberá Indians

Other beautiful native handicrafts are represented by tightly woven baskets made from the fronds of the chunga palm. They take several days to a month to weave and are dyed with materials extracted from tropical fruits and trees. The Ngobe-Buglé people weave *chacara* bags from the leaves of the wild pineapple plant. These practical bags are used for transporting everything from babies to market goods. They are a popular tourist item.

Life Is Exciting

F AR AND WIDE, THE CITIZENS OF PANAMA ARE A GENTLE AND courteous people. They possess a warm sense of humor and greet strangers with a firm handshake. They love to celebrate holidays and festivals. Eating is a national pastime, and the variety of foods is seemingly endless. Panamanians often are night owls who dance the night away at local discos and nightclubs. They are an active and athletic people who participate well in many sports. Driving may be their favorite outdoor activity, and Panamanian traffic is not recommended for timid drivers.

Opposite: **A group of schoolboys have some fun before a soccer game.**

Social Characteristics

Panamanians are a very friendly people. When meeting friends or strangers, men almost always shake hands. Women who are greeting friends or relatives frequently exchange a light kiss on the cheek. If women are not acquainted, they may pat each other on the arm. If there is a group of people, it is considered rude not to personally greet each person. In rural areas, residents nod or give a verbal greeting as they pass on the street, even to strangers. When you are a guest in a Panamanian home, it is considered polite to give the host or hostess a small gift.

The first time that professional men and women meet, they usually exchange business cards. Titles are important to Panamanians. *Licenciado* (university degree), *ingeniero* (engineer), and *doctor* (an advanced degree) are used on business cards and when signing letters. Teachers are respected in

Public Holidays in Panama

Fixed Dates for Public Holidays

New Year's Day	January 1
Martyrs' Day	January 9
Labor Day	May 1
Father's Day	June 16
Anniversary of Separation from Colombia	November 3
Flag Day	November 4
Colón Day (Colón only)	November 5
Anniversary of the first Call for Independence in Los Santos	November 10
Anniversary of Independence from Spain	November 28
Mother's Day	December 8
Christmas Day	December 25

Movable Dates for Public Holidays

Carnival (2 days)	February or March
Ash Wednesday	February or March
Holy Thursday to Easter Sunday (4 days)	March or April

Panamanian society and are regarded as citizens of status.

Let's Eat

Eating is seldom boring in Panama. A considerable variety of food is available. In the countryside, typical Panamanian dishes are dominant. Rice is served with almost every meal. Meat and seafood dishes make up the main course. Sea bass is the most popular seafood, although shrimp is found on almost every menu. Chicken and beef are served everywhere. Children especially love *empanadas*, which are deep fried dough stuffed with cheese or meat. *Chicha* is a popular, refreshing drink made from a variety of fresh fruit mixed with water, sugar,

Panama's variety of foods abounds.

Typical Foods

Tortillas served at breakfast are circular, 0.5-inch- (1.25-cm-) thick pieces of corn dough. They are deep fried and served with melted cheese on top. *Arroz con guandu* is Panama's most popular side dish. It is rice cooked with beans. *Sancocho* is the national dish. It is a hearty soup made with chicken, onions, oregano leaves, green peppers, *ñamé* (yam), and the herb *cilantro*. *Petacones* are eaten as snacks. They are thinly sliced green plantains (a banana type of fruit) that are deep fried and salted. Flan, a light egg custard with caramel sauce, is Panama's favorite dessert.

and ice. Adults almost always relax with a cup of rich Panamanian coffee after a meal.

Panama City is famous for its international food choices. There are five-star French and Italian restaurants as well as Middle Eastern, Indian, Chinese, Japanese, Greek, and other cultural food specialties. The evening meal usually begins late, after 9:00 P.M., and may last two or three hours. Conversation is an important part of the eating experience. The topics usually include sports, food, the weather, politics, or what the speaker would do if he or she won the national lottery. In many of the larger restaurants, entertainment is provided during the meal. Musicians may sing songs about life and love, or dancers may perform the tamborito.

After dinner Panamanians head for the discos, nightclubs, and casinos. The pulse of the city can be felt at the entrances of the vibrant nightspots. Salsa bands hammer out the rhythms of Panama's distinct music. The discos remain open all night, and dawn frequently greets the most dedicated dancers as they leave the clubs. Music and dancing are major recreations in Panama.

Taking a Chance

The National Lottery for the Benefit of Panama was founded in 1883. The lottery is one of the most popular activities in Panama. Vendors, who are government employees, sell lottery tickets on the busy streets of the cities and in rural areas. Many Panamanians buy lottery tickets every week of the year. Prizes range from one dollar to several thousand dollars. The lottery is well liked because the government requires that 64 percent of all ticket sales be paid out as prize money to the lucky winners.

Testing Physical Skills

Baseball is the most popular sport in Panama. Although girls play baseball in school, it is the boys who dominate the sport. Boys start playing baseball at a very early age. They play ball during recess at school, after school, and on weekends. Many boys participate in formal Junior League competitions. Panama's National Junior League team has played in regional and international Junior League World Series tournaments.

Panamanian baseball players are well known for their speed and hitting ability. Baseball scouts from major league teams in the United States frequently

Panama's Dimerson Nunez gets tagged out during the pre-Olympic tournament in Panama 2003.

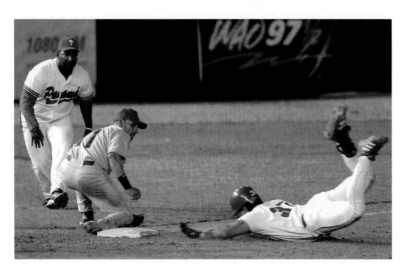

visit Panama looking for new talent. Since 1955, more than forty Panamanian baseball players have played for professional teams in the United States. Some of the best-known players include Rod Carew, Juan Berenguer, Bruce Chen, Manny Sanguillen, and Mariano Rivera. Rivera has earned legendary status as a relief pitcher for the New York Yankees. In 1999 he was voted the Most Valuable Player in the World Series of Baseball.

Panama's Mariano Rivera throws a pitch in the ninth inning of a Yankee game.

Mr. Baseball

Rodney Cline Carew (Rod Carew) is a national hero in Panama. He was born on a train in the Panama Canal Zone in 1945. His family moved to New York City in 1961. He began his professional career in 1967 with the Minnesota Twins and was named American League Rookie of the Year. Carew was one of the best hitters in baseball for many years. His batting average was above .300 in fifteen consecutive seasons. In 1977 he batted .388 and was selected as the Most Valuable Player in the American League. He won seven batting titles and had a total of 3,053 hits during his career with the Minnesota Twins and the California Angels. In 1991 Rod Carew was elected and inducted into the Baseball Hall of Fame in Cooperstown, New York. The national baseball stadium in Panama City is named Rod Carew Stadium.

Locals surf off of Panama's beaches.

In recent years, soccer has been the fastest growing sport in Panama. Soccer is popular throughout Latin America, and many cities and towns in Panama have established soccer clubs and sponsor tournaments. Panamanian men love to attend boxing matches and cockfights as social outlets and opportunities to gamble. Since most Panamanians live within an hour's drive of some of the world's most beautiful beaches, water sports are very popular with families. Swimming, snorkeling, surfing, fishing, and scuba diving draw thousands of participants who cherish the opportunity to escape the hustle and bustle of city life.

Manos de Piedra (Hands of Stone)

Roberto Duran is considered to have been the best lightweight boxer in the history of the sport. He was born in Guarare, Panama, in 1951. Duran fought his first professional fight when he was sixteen. He fought and lost his last professional fight when he was fifty. After winning the lightweight title in 1972, he successfully defended the title twelve consecutive times. In eleven of his twelve title defenses, he knocked out his opponent. During a career that spanned four decades, he won world championships as a lightweight, welterweight, light middleweight, junior middleweight, and middleweight. His final professional record was 104 victories, 16 defeats, and 69 knockouts.

A jeep travels along the Pan-American Highway.

Exploring the Country

Cars and buses are the major means of transportation in Panama. Panama's 7,203 miles (11,590 km) of roadways, of which 2,535 miles (4,079 km) are paved (35 percent), provide adequate access to most parts of the country. The two most important highways are the Pan-American Highway and the Trans-Isthmian Highway. The Trans-Isthmian Highway runs parallel to the Panama Canal and connects Panama City with Colón.

The Pan-American Highway is one of the most famous roads in the world. It is a vast linkage of highways that stretch more than 16,000 miles (25,744 km) from Alaska to southern Argentina. In Panama, the Pan-American Highway runs 339 miles (543 km) from the border with Costa Rica deep into the Darién rain forest. Dense jungle and extensive swamps have prevented completion of the last 54 miles (87 km) of the Pan-

The diablos rojos, or red devils, are a colorful way to get around Panama City.

American Highway between Panama and Colombia. Environmentalists would like to prevent the completion of the highway to protect the natural surroundings and the indigenous people of the region.

The public bus system in Panama is well established. Reliable and safe service connects most of rural Panama with the major urban centers. A truly hair-raising experience awaits the brave visitor willing to ride the *diablos rojos* (red devils) of Panama City. The red devils are brightly painted former U.S. school buses. They frequently have pictures of famous movie stars and musicians like Ruben Blades, Mel Gibson, and Julia Roberts painted on their sides. The buses roar through the streets of Panama City blaring popular salsa music through powerful loudspeakers.

Driving a car in Panama requires considerable skill. Streets often are poorly maintained. There are few place signs, traffic signals are scarce, and city traffic is congested. Many drivers are badly trained, undisciplined, and aggressive. The unwritten rule of the road seems to be, "He who goes the fastest and has the most nerve, wins!"

The Panama Canal, Panama Railroad, and the country's major highways have made Panama a true crossroads of international activity. The rich diversity of ethnic groups with their multitude of cultural characteristics has created a true melting pot of social expression. Panama's history reveals a fascinating linkage of great events and a powerful people. Panama is a nation whose past has shaped its present, while its citizens focus on a future filled with hope.

Timeline

Panamanian History

The first Native Americans arrive in Panama.   12,000–10,000 B.C.

Spanish explorer Rodrigo de Bastidas "discovers" Panama.   A.D. 1501

Christopher Columbus explores Panama on his fourth voyage to the New World.   1502

Antigua is founded as the first European settlement in Central America.   1510

Vasco Núñez de Balboa discovers the Pacific Ocean.   1513

Panama City is founded by Pedro Arias Dávila.   1519

Spaniards led by Francisco Pizarro conquer the Incas.   1532

Construction of fortifications at Portobelo are started.   1597

British buccaneer Sir Henry Morgan sacks Panama City.   1671

World History

2500 B.C.   Egyptians build the Pyramids and the Sphinx in Giza.

563 B.C.   The Buddha is born in India.

A.D. 313   The Roman emperor Constantine recognizes Christianity.

610   The Prophet Muhammad begins preaching a new religion called Islam.

1054   The Eastern (Orthodox) and Western (Roman) Churches break apart.

1066   William the Conqueror defeats the English in the Battle of Hastings.

1095   Pope Urban II proclaims the First Crusade.

1215   King John seals the Magna Carta.

1300s   The Renaissance begins in Italy.

1347   The Black Death sweeps through Europe.

1453   Ottoman Turks capture Constantinople, conquering the Byzantine Empire.

1492   Columbus arrives in North America.

1500s   The Reformation leads to the birth of Protestantism.

1776   The Declaration of Independence is signed.

1789   The French Revolution begins.

Panamanian History

Simón Bolívar and General Fransico de Paula Santander defeat Spanish forces at Boyacá.	1819
Formation of the Republic of Gran Colombia.	1821
The Republic of New Granada is formed.	1831
Construction of the Panama Railroad takes place.	1850–1855
Lieutenant Lucien Napoleon Bonaparte Wyse secures a treaty with Colombia for the French to build a canal in Panama.	1878
The Republic of Colombia is formed.	1886
Ferdinand-Marie de Lesseps leads a French attempt to excavate a canal in Panama.	1880–1888
The Thousand Day War is fought.	1899–1902
Panama declares independence from Colombia. The Hay–Bunau-Varilla Treaty is signed in Washington, DC.	1903
The United States constructs the Panama Canal.	1904–1914
President José Antonio Remón is assassinated.	1955
Anti-American riots in Panama cause more than twenty deaths.	1964
Brigadier General Omar Torrijos Herrera establishes a military dictatorship.	1968
Torrijos negotiates a new Panama Canal Treaty with the United States.	1977
Torrijos is killed in an airplane crash. Manuel Noriega assumes power in Panama.	1981
Noriega is ousted by the U.S. military in "Operation Just Cause."	1989
The United States returns sovereignty of the canal to Panama; Mireya Elisa Moscoso Rodríguez is elected first female president of Panama.	1999
Martín Torrijos Espino, son of Brigadier General Omar Torrijos, is elected president of Panama.	2004

World History

1865	The American Civil War ends.
1914	World War I breaks out.
1917	The Bolshevik Revolution brings communism to Russia.
1929	Worldwide economic depression begins.
1939	World War II begins, following the German invasion of Poland.
1945	World War II ends.
1957	The Vietnam War starts.
1969	Humans land on the moon.
1975	The Vietnam War ends.
1979	Soviet Union invades Afghanistan.
1983	Drought and famine in Africa.
1989	The Berlin Wall is torn down, as communism crumbles in Eastern Europe.
1991	Soviet Union breaks into separate states.
1992	Bill Clinton is elected U.S. president.
2000	George W. Bush is elected U.S. president.
2001	Terrorists attack World Trade Towers, New York and the Pentagon, Washington, D.C.
2003	Coalition of forty-nine nations, headed by the United States and Great Britain, invade Iraq.

Fast Facts

Official name: República de Panamá (Republic of Panama)

Capital: Panama City

Official language: Spanish

Panama City

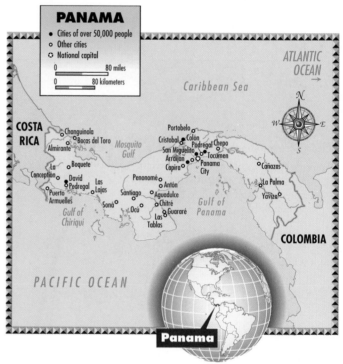

Panama's flag

Quetzal

Official religion:	none
Year of founding:	1903
National anthem:	"Himno Istmeño" ("Isthmus Anthem")
Government:	Constitutional Democracy (Republic)
Chief of state:	President
Area:	30,193 square miles (78,200 sq km)
Coordinates of geographic center:	9° north latitude, 80° west longitude
Highest elevation:	Barú Volcano (Volcán Barú), 11,401 feet (3,475 m) above sea level
Lowest elevation:	Sea level along the Caribbean and Pacific coastlines
Average temperature:	81°F (27°C)
Average precipitation:	126 inches (320 cm) on the Caribbean coast, 75 inches (190 cm) on the Pacific coast
National population (2004 est.):	3,120,000

Population of major cities (2004 est):

Panama City	463,093
San Miguelito	314,000
Colón	175,000
David	125,000
Tocumen	90,000
Arraiján	69,100

Panama Canal

Currency

Famous landmarks: ▶ *Darién National Park*

▶ *Gatún Lake*

▶ *Panama Canal*

▶ *Panama Canal Museum*, Panama City

▶ *Panama Viejo*, near Panama City

▶ *Portobelo*

▶ *San Blas Islands*

Industry: The industrial sector of Panama's economy is poorly developed. Less than 20 percent of the labor force is employed in industry. The most common manufacturing activities are food processing and beverage production for local markets. Hydroelectric generation produces approximately 50 percent of Panama's electrical demand. Although Panama has large copper deposits, mining is largely insignificant in the country's economy.

Currency: Panama uses U.S. paper currency as its basic currency, but calls the bills balboas. Panama mints its own coins, which are the same size as U.S. coins but are called centavos. Panamanian currency is equal in value to all U.S. currency.

Weights and measures: Both the metric and imperial systems of weights and measures are used in Panama.

Literacy rate: 92.6 percent

Black Panamanian

Ruben Blades

Common Spanish words and phrases:

Adiós.	Good bye.
Buenos días.	Good morning.
Buenas noches.	Good night/evening.
Como está usted?	How are you?
Cuánto?	How much?
Dónde ésta?	Where is …?
Habla usted español?	Do you speak Spanish?
Gracias.	Thank you.
Por favor.	Please.
Qué hora es?	What time is it?

Famous Panamanians:

Pedro Arias Dávila (1440–1531)
Spanish governor of Panama

Vasco Núñez de Balboa (1475–1519)
Spanish explorer

Ruben Blades (1948–)
Singer, actor, political activist

Rodney Cline Carew (1945–)
Baseball player

Dr. Manuel Amador Guerrero (1833–1909)
First president of Panama

General Omar Torrijos Herrera (1929–1981)
Military dictator

To Find Out More

Nonfiction

▶ Keller, Ulrich. *The Building of the Panama Canal in Historic Photographs*. Toronto: General Publishing Company, 1983.

▶ McNeese, Tim. *The Panama Canal* (Building History Series). San Diego: Lucent Books, 1997.

Hispanic Biographies

▶ Cruz, Barbara C. *Ruben Blades: Salsa Singer and Social Activist*. Berkeley Heights, CA: Enslow Publishers, Inc., 1997.

Videos

▶ *Panama Canal*. Kaw Valley Films and Video, Shawnee, Kansas, 2001.

▶ *Panama: Wild Rain Forest of Life*. National Geographic Society, Washington, DC, 2000.

Web Sites

▶ **Panama Map**
http://www.lonelyplanet.com/
mapshells/central_america/panama/
panama.htm
*Students can take a tour of the country
and read descriptions of places by click-
ing on geographical locations.*

▶ **Panama Canal**
http://www.canalmuseum.com/
*The very best Internet site available for
photos, documents, stories, books, and
links regarding the Panama Canal.*

Embassy

▶ **Embassy of the Republic of
Panama**
2862 McGill Terrace, NW
Washington, DC 20008
(202) 483-1407

Index

Page numbers in *italics* indicate illustrations.

A

agriculture, 21, 35, 81–83
All Soul's Day, 100
Amador, Manuel, 65, 114
Amistad National Park, 38
animal life. *See* wildlife
Antigua, 43–45
Arias Madrid, Arnulfo, 57
art. *See* culture
Atahualpa, 44, *44*

B

Balboa, Vasco Núñez de, *43*, 43–44, *114*
Balboa and the Gold, 9
Balladares, Ernesto Pérez, 60
banana production, *82*, 82–83
Barro Colorado Island, 25, 38–39
Barro Colorado Nature Monument, 38
Barú Volcano, 18, *18*
baseball, *122*, 122–123, *123*
Bastidas, Rodrigo de, 42
Bidlack, Benjamin, 48
Biosphere Reserve, 37–38
birdlife, *32*, 32–33, *33*
Black Christ of Portobelo, *100*, 100–103
Blades, Ruben, 111, 112, *112*
Bocas del Toro Islands, 22, 23
Bolívar, Simón, 47–48, *48*, 50
Bolivia, 45
Boquete, 23–24, 26–27
Bunau-Varilla, Philippe, 53

Bush, George H.W., 59–60
bushmaster, 31, *31*

C

Canal Zone, 38, 54, 56
Carew, Rodney Cline, 123, *123*
Cerro Punta, 81, *81*
Cerro Rico Mountains, 45
Chagres National Park, 38
Chagres River, 25, 38, 55
Charles V, 50
Chinatown, 92, *92*
Chinese New Year celebration, *92*
Chiriquí Province, 86, *86*
Church of San Felipe, 100
Church of San José, 99, *99*
Church of the Gold Altar, 99, *99*
City of Eternal Spring, The, 24
civil war, 52
climate, 21, 23–25
Coiba Island, 21
Coiba Island National Park, 38
Colón, 25, 26, *26*, 49
Colón Free Trade Zone, 79
Columbia, 48
Columbus, Christopher, 42, *42*
container ship in the Panama Canal, *73*
coral reefs, 35
Cordillera Central, 18, *18*
Corpus Christi festival, *108*
corruption, 57, 68, 75

crafts. *See* handicrafts
crops, 21, 81–83
Culebra Cut, 19, *19, 51*, 55, *55*
culture. *See also* lifestyle
    arts and literature, 114
    dance, 111–113
    family, 109, *109*
    folklore, 110–111
    handicrafts, 115–117, *116, 117*
    Kuna Indians, 91, *91*
    languages, 93, 94
    marriage customs, 90, 110
    music, 111, 112
    Native American protection, 90
    social characteristics, 119–120
currency, 74, *74*

D

Darién National Park, *37*, 37–39
Darién Province, 86
Dávila, Pedro Arias, *44*, 44–45
deforestation, 29, 36, *36*
Don Bosco Basilica, 98
Drake, Francis, *40*
drug-trafficking, 58–60, 75, 86
Duran, Roberto, 124, *124*

E

eagle, harpy, 33, *33*
economy
    banking, 73–75
    effects of Panama Canal, 11
    and environmental concerns, 36–37
    and foreign relations, 69
    free trade zone, 79
    Panama Canal, 77, *77*
    tourism, 75–76, *76*
education, 94–95
El Carmen Church, 98

Emberá baskets, 117, *117*
Emberá woman, 90
Enciso, Martín Fernández de, 42–43
Endara, Guillermo, 60
environmental concerns, 29, 36–37, 60,
    83, 127

F

farming, 21, 81–83
Feast of the Black Christ, *101*, 101–103,
    102
Federal Family Code, 90
fishing, 35, 83
Flower and Coffee Festival, 27
folk dance
    congo, 113, *113*
    tamborito, 111–113
forest reserves, 37–39
forests. *See* mangrove forests; rain forests
France, 10, 50–51
Franklin, Benjamin, 50

G

Gaillard Cut. *See* Culebra Cut
Gatún Dam, 55
Gatún Lake, 25, 38, 39, 55
geography
    borders, 15
    coastal lowlands, *20*, 20–21, *21*
    features of Panama, 17
    geological formation, 15
    islands, 21–23, *22*
    map, *17*
    mountains, 17–19, *18*
    size and location, 15–17
Goethals, George Washington, 55–56
gold trade, 46–47
Gorgas, William Crawford, 54–55

government
    constitution, 97
    corruption, 57, 68
    democracy, 60–69
    dictatorship, 57–60
    Electoral Tribunal, 66
    executive branch, 63–65
    Federal Family Code, 90
    foreign relations, 69
    independence from Columbia, 10–11, 52–53
    independence from Spain, 47–48
    judicial branch, 67–68
    law enforcement, 68, 68–69
    legislative branch, 65, 65–67
    nationalism, 56
    19th century unrest, 52
    Panamanian Defense Forces (PDF), 57, 58
    political divisions, 67
    political instability, 56
Guerrero, Manuel Amador, 53
Gulf of Chiriquí, 20
Gulf of Panama, 20

H

handicrafts, 90, 115–117, *116*, *117*
harpy eagle, 33, *33*
Hay-Bunau-Varilla Treaty, *53*, 53–54, 56
Hay-Herran Treaty, 52–53
healthcare/health issues, 30–31, 32, 51
holidays, national/public, 56, 120
holidays, religious, 100, 101–103, 107
Holy Ghost orchid, 30
House of Worship, 105, 107
hydroelectric power, 25, 80

I

Incas/Incan Empire, 44, *44*, 45

industry
    agriculture, 21, 81–83
    banking, 73–75
    fishing, 35, 83
    hydroelectric power, 25, 80
    manufacturing, 80, 81
    mining, 81, 83
    tourism, 26–27, 75–76, *76*, 78, 91
insects, 31–32, *32*
Isthmus of Panama, 8, 9
Ivaldi, Humberto, 114

J

jaguarundi, *34*
Jaramillo Levi, Enrique, 114

K

Keith, Minor C., 82
Kuna Indians, 22, *22*, 91, *91*, 116–117

L

languages, 93, 94
law enforcement, 68, 68–69
Lesseps, Ferdinand-Marie de, *50*, 50–51
Lewis, Roberto, 114
lifestyle. *See also* culture
    food/meals, *120*, 120–121
    nightlife, 121
    social characteristics, 119–120
    sports, 122–124
literacy, 94–95
literature. *See* culture
lottery, 122

M

Madden Dam, 80, *80*
malaria, 32, 51, 54–55
mammals, 34, *34*
mangrove forests, 35

Manzanillo Island, 26
maps
    Colonial Latin America, *47*
    ethnic distribution, 86
    geographical, *17*
    geopolitical, *13*
    Panama Canal, *54*
    Panama City, *71*
    Panama's provinces, *67*
    population density, *85*
    resources, *82*
    Spanish settlement, *41*
marine life, 35
Martyr's Day, 56
medicines/health care, 30–31
mestiza girl, *87*
military
    National Guard, 57
    Panamanian Defense Forces (PDF),
        57, 58
    Panamanian Public Forces, 69
Miró, Ricardo, 114
mola, *116*, 116–117
Morgan, Henry, *46*, 46–47
Moscoso Rodríguez, Mireya Elisa, 60, *61*
Mosquera, Tomás Cipriano de, 48
mosquitoes, *32*, *32*, 51, 54–55
mountains, 17–19, *18*
mudflats, 20, *20*
Mutual Legal Assistance Treaty, 75

N

National Fair of Crafts, 115
National Guard, 57
national parks, 21, *37*, 37–39
national symbols
    bird, 33, *33*
    dance, 111–113
    flag, 65, *65*
    flower, 30
    food, 121
    poet, 114
natural resources
    and deforestation, 36–37
    fishing, 35
    hydroelectric power, 25, 80
    map, *82*
    mining, 81
New Granada, 47
Nicuesa, Diego de, 42
Noriega, Manuel, *58*, 58–60
Nunez, Dimerson, *122*

O

oil tanker at Miraflores lock, *55*
orchids, 30

P

Panama Canal, *11*
    construction by France, 50–51
    construction by United States, 52–56
    Culebra Cut, 19, *19*, *51*, 55, *55*
    and deforestation, 37
    French construction/excavation, 10, *10*
    improvements and modernization,
        76–77, *77*
    Panamanian sovereignity, 58, 60
    recruitment of workers, 88
    river system, 25, 38
Panama Canal Museum, 115, *115*
Panama City, *16*, 25, 45, 46–47, 70,
    70–71
Panama City Cathedral, 96
Panamanian Defense Forces (PDF),
    57, 58
Panamanian Public Forces, 69
Panama Railroad, 19, 20, 48–49, *49*,
    78, *78*

Pan-American Highway, *125*, 125–127
parrots, *28*
Pearl Islands, 22, *22*
Pedro the Cruel, *44*, 44–45
people. *See also* population
    Chinese, 92
    earliest settlers, 41
    Emberá tribe, 117
    ethnic diversity, 87–89
    Kuna Indians, 22, *22*, *35*, 66, 91, *91*,
        116–117
    Native Americans, 89–92
    Ngobe-Buglé tribe, 117
    Spanish explorers, 9, 9–10, 41–42, *43*,
        43–47
    Wounaan tribe, 117
Peregrine Pearl, 22
Peru, 45, 47, *47*
Pizarro, Francisco, 43, 44, *44*
plant life, 29–31, 39
police force. *See* law enforcement
pollera, 116, *116*
population. *See also* people
    density, *85*, 85–86
    ethnic diversity, 87–89
    major cities, 89
    national, 85
    racial discrimination, 88–89
    16th century, 41
Portobelo, 45, *45*
Portobelo National Park, 38

Q

quetzal, 33, *33*

R

racial discrimination, 88–89
rainfall, 24–25
rain forests, 21, *29*, 29–31, 36–37,
    38–39, *39*
red devils, *126*, 127
religion
    Baha'i, 105, 107
    Black Christ of Portobelo, *100*,
        100–103
    Chinese, 104
    Evangelical, 103–104
    holidays, 100, 101–103, 107
    House of Worship, 105, 107
    Islam, 104
    Jewish, 105
    Mormon, 104
    Protestant, 103–104
    Roman Catholic, 97–100
    Santería, *106*, 107
Remón, José Antonio, 56
Republic of Columbia, 48
Republic of Gran Colombia, 48
Republic of New Granada, 48
Rivera, Mariano, 123, *123*
rivers/river systems, 25, 38
Roosevelt, Theodore, 11, 52

S

San Blas Islands, 22, *22*
Santander, Francisco de Paula, 48
Santiago, 27
scarecrows, *110*, 110–111
schoolchildren, 95, *118*

science/scientific research, 38–39
Serranía del Darién, 19
ship registrations/shipping, *79*, 79–80
silver trade, 46–47
sloth, *34*
Smithsonian Institute, 38
soccer, 124
Spanish explorers, 9, 9–10, *43*, 43–47
sports, 122–124
Stevens, John, 55–56

T
Thousand Day War, The, 52
tides/tidewaters, 20, *20*
timeline, 128–129
Torrijos Espino, Martín, 61, 64, *64*
Torrijos Herrera, Omar, *57*, 57–58
toucan, 32
tourism, 26–27, 75–76, *76*, 78, 91
trade, 11, 45, 46–47, 73
Trans-Isthmian Highway, 125
transportation. *See also* Panama Canal
    bus system, *126*, 127
    Pan-American Highway, *125*,
        125–127
    railroad, 19, 20, 48–49, *49*, 78, *78*
    roadways, 125–127
    Trans-Isthmian Highway, 125
trees. *See* plant life

U
United Fruit Company, 23, 82–83
United Nations, 69

United Nations Educational, Scientific
    and Cultural Organization
        (UNESCO), 38
United States
    Central Intelligence Agency (CIA),
        58–60
    Hay-Bunau-Varilla Treaty, 53–54, 56
    Hay-Herran Treaty, 52–53
    and Manuel Noriega, 58–60
    military, *59*, 59–60
    National Cancer Institute, 31
    Operation Just Cause, 59–60
    Panama Railroad, 48–49, *49*
    and Panama's independence, 52–53
    purchase of Canal construction
        rights, 51
universities, 95

V
vegetable ivory, 117
Venezuela, 48
Vernon, Edward, 45
Volcán Barú, 18, *18*

W
water sports, 124
weights and measures, 79
wildlife, 31–34
wildlife sanctuaries, 37–39
World Heritage Sites, 38
Wyse, Lucien Napoleon Bonaparte, 50

Y
yellow fever, 32, 51, 54–55

Meet the Author

Byron Augustin is a professor of geography at Texas State University in San Marcos, Texas. His love for geography has instilled in him a passion for traveling abroad whenever he has an opportunity to do so. He has visited forty-nine of the fifty United States, twenty-six of Mexico's thirty-one states, and eight of Canada's ten provinces. Dr. Augustin has toured fifty-four countries on five of the seven continents.

Byron Augustin is an avid professional photographer. More than 1,100 of his photos have been published worldwide. The National Geographic Society, *Encyclopedia Britannica*, *Outdoor Life*, and scores of books and magazines have published his photographs. More than a dozen books in the Enchantment of the World series feature his photos. He is the author of Enchantment of the World *Bolivia* and the *United Arab Emirates*.

Writing the book on Panama was a special treat. Dr. Augustin teaches a course on the geography of Latin America and has been reading about and doing research on Panama for more than thirty years. To write this book, he used the superb library facilities on his own university campus as well as the New Braunfels Public Library. He also surfed the Internet and reviewed 110 years of *National Geographic Magazine*. Much of the statistical data was provided by Panamanian government agencies during his January 2004 visit to Panama.

Augustin feels that it is difficult to write about a country without visiting it personally. He made two visits to Panama to prepare for writing this book. During a recent visit he rented a car and traveled with a professional guide across much of Panama. Their trip took them to the Azuero Peninsula, the high volcanic mountains of western Panama, and most of the country's major cities. He took a boat trip through the Panama Canal, rode the historic Panama Railroad from Panama City to Colón, and hired a pilot to fly him over historic sites, Panama City, and the major locks on the Panama Canal. He dined on some of the best food he has ever eaten and marveled at the cultural and physical diversity of this small energetic nation, known as the Crossroads of the World.

Photo Credits

Photographs © 2005:

AP/Wide World Photos: 102 (Kathryn Cook), 98 bottom, 122 bottom (Arnulfo Franco), 61, 112, 133 bottom (Tomas Munita), 123 top, (Kathy Willens), 78 (Jaime E. Yau)

Bruce Coleman Inc./Michael DeFreitas: 2

Byron Augustin: 20, 27, 45, 55 bottom, 81, 90, 105, 110, 114, 115, 117, 122 top

Corbis Images: 95 (Paul Almasy), 96 (Morton Beebe), 42, 43, 48, 124 bottom (Bettmann), 62 (Keith Dannemiller), 116 bottom (Randy Faris), 31, 33 right, 34 top, 131 (Michael & Patricia Fogden), 57 (Lou Garcia/Bettmann), 58 (Bill Gentile), 32 bottom (Gavriel Jecan), 22 bottom, 76, 113, 126 (Wolfgang Kaehler), 106 (Daniel Lainé), cover, 6, 7 top, 12, 14, 16, 18, 19, 21, 22 top, 26, 39, 70, 77, 80, 91 left, 91 right, 109, 118, 130 left, 132 top, 120 (Danny Lehman), 8 (NASA), 125 (Tim Page), 79 (Sergio Pitamitz), 123 bottom (Neal Preston), 101 (Reuters), 35 (David Samuel Robbins), 29, 72 (Paul A. Souders), 9 (Stapleton Collection), 59 (Les Stone), 49, 51, 53, 55 top

Hulton | Archive/Getty Images: 44 bottom

Kevin Schafer: 34 bottom

Mary Evans Picture Library: 31 (Douglas McCarthy), 10, 37

Peter Arnold Inc.: 88, 133 top (Susan Pierres), 36 (Stuart G.R. Warner/UNEP)

Reuters: 66 (Eliana Aponte), 33 left, 64, 68, 82 top, 92, 100 (Alberto Lowe)

South American Pictures: 7 bottom, 116 top, 124 top (Mike Harding), 25, 37 (Tony Morrison)

The Art Archive/Picture Desk: 44 top (Museé Rochelle/Dagli Orti), 50 (Dagli Orti)

The Image Works: 32 top (Jack Clark), 11 (Jon Mitchell)

Victor Englebert: 18, 24, 65, 73, 74, 84, 86 top, 87, 93, 98 top, 99, 108, 132 bottom

Maps by XNR Productions Inc.